100 Bible Questions and Answers on Prophecy and the End Times

Alex McFarland
& Bert Harper

BroadStreet
PUBLISHING

BroadStreet Publishing® Group, LLC
Savage, Minnesota, USA
BroadStreetPublishing.com

100 Bible Questions and Answers on Prophecy and the End Times

9781424570331 (softcover)
9781424570348 (ebook)

Cover and interior by Garborg Design Works | garborgdesign.com

Printed in the USA

25 26 27 28 29 5 4 3 2 1

CONTENTS

Section 3: The Role of Israel and Bible Prophecy

Section 4: Views of the Rapture

Section 5: The Antichrist and the False Prophet

Section 6: The Tribulation

Section 7: God's Future Judgments

Section 8: The Second Coming and the Millennial Kingdom

Section 9: The New Heavens and New Earth

Section 10: Technology and the End Times

INTRODUCTION

Why Does the Bible Contain Prophecy?

It has often been said of biblical prophecy, "Only God writes history in advance." This, of course, is a reference to the Bible's prophetic passages, which time and again have proven accurate regarding future events. The late Dr. H. L. Willmington, a prolific author and renowned Bible scholar, wrote: "One of the acid tests of any religion is its ability to predict the future. In this area (as in all other areas) the Bible reigns supreme. One searches in vain through the pages of other sacred writings to find even a single line of accurate prophecy."[1]

The Bible contains roughly 26.8 percent prophecy. According to the *Encyclopedia of Biblical Prophecy* by J. Barton Payne, there are 1,239 prophecies in the Old Testament and 578 prophecies in the New Testament. This makes a total of 1,817 prophecies. These prophecies are contained in 8,352 of the Bible verses. Given that there are 31,124 verses in the entire Bible, the eight-thousand-plus verses containing prophecy constitute just under 27 percent of the Bible's volume.[2] And what has Scripture accurately predicted—often centuries in advance—that later came true? A very short list of fulfilled prophecies would include

- that Israel would spend four hundred years captive in Egypt (Genesis 15:13);

1 Harold L. Willmington, *12 Essential Doctrines: Systematic Theology* (Lynchburg, VA: Liberty Home Bible Institute, 2014), 71.

2 J. Barton Payne, *Encyclopedia of Biblical Prophecy* (New York: Harper & Row, 2020), 674–75.

- that the descendants of Ishmael would struggle against the children of Isaac— and ultimately, the whole world (Genesis 16:12);
- that Israel would spend seventy years captive in Babylon (Jeremiah 25:11; 29:10);
- and that the Jewish people would one day be scattered throughout the nations (Leviticus 26:33; Deuteronomy 28:64);
- That Israel would be reborn, and Jews would return to their ancient homeland in the end times, just before the return of Christ (Deuteronomy 30:3; Ezekiel 36–39);
- That in the last days, God would plant the Israelites back in the land of their fathers (Jeremiah 24:6);
- That Israel would rebuild the ancient cities (Isaiah 61:4);
- That Israel would one day turn the desert into a blossoming garden (Isaiah 51:3);
- That God would increase the population of the Jews (Ezekiel 37:26).

Other Prophecies

Around 590 BC, the prophet Ezekiel made some startlingly clear predictions about the city of Tyre (one of the world's oldest metropolises, with a population of thirty thousand at the time of Ezekiel). Biblical prophets warned that the Lord would bring judgment upon Tyre. Several nations were to attack Tyre, like ocean waves beating on the seashore (Ezekiel 26:3).

It was prophesied that the city of Tyre would be captured by the Babylonian king Nebuchadnezzar, multiple other nations would participate in its destruction, its foundations would be leveled, the stones and lumber of the city would be thrown into the ocean, and that this great city would never be rebuilt as it was (cf. Ezekiel 26:2–14; Jeremiah 47:4; Isaiah 23:1, 11; Zechariah 9:4). All of this (and more) came true centuries after God's prophets initially foretold it.

In the birth, life, death, and resurrection of Jesus Christ (*Yeshua*, in Hebrew) at least three hundred prophecies were fulfilled. God's past record of absolute accuracy regarding the first coming of the Messiah (and other world events) means that we may fully trust Scripture regarding Jesus' second coming and future events.

HOLY BIBLE, BOOK DIVINE

We believe that compelling lines of evidence indicate that the Bible is of divine origin. As such, God's Word informs us about past history, provides salvific truth regarding our soul's destiny, and has much to say about this planet's future.

There are prophecies about moral and spiritual trends. There are prophecies about weather patterns. There are prophecies about people groups and specific countries. There are prophecies about followers of Jesus, whom the Bible calls "the church."

There are prophecies about demonic activity that will escalate near the conclusion of history and the time of Christ's return. And with sobering clarity, the Bible lays out prophecies about the Jewish people, their persecution, and the nation of Israel. From early in the twentieth century to the present moment in the twenty-first, we believe that humans live in the times of the fulfillment of ancient prophecies.

The prophetic accuracy of the Bible represents knowledge of world events that mere mortals could not have possessed.

What Is Eschatology and Why Does It Matter?

Scholars speak of general eschatology and of personal eschatology. What does this mean? *Eschatology* is the study of "last things," the "end of time." General eschatology asks, "What is going to happen, ultimately, to the world?" Short answer: Christ is coming back to reign in righteousness! But consider the issue we all must face: personal eschatology. This is the question, "What is going to happen, ultimately, to me?"

In considering what the Bible says about human destiny and the future, let us not forget the most pressing matter of all: our soul's destiny and the need to be sure that we're in a right relationship with Christ. This, really, is the purpose of this book.

As We Begin Our Study of Prophecy and the End Times

In our previous books, *100 Bible Questions and Answers* and *100 Bible Questions and Answers for Families*, we were overwhelmed by the responses from many of our readers. For over a decade, we have been privileged to host the radio show "Exploring the Word" on American Family Radio. After the publication of our book, we heard from many readers about the ways God used the biblical responses to help them in their walk with God and as a tool for them to help others.

As we reflected on new areas to explore, we hit upon the subject of Bible prophecy. Our turbulent world includes conflict in the Middle East, increased globalism, and changes in our own nation that have fueled discussion about the end times like never before in our culture.

Just before we began writing this book, Hamas launched a brutal attack on Israel on October 7, 2023, resulting in twelve hundred Israeli casualties. Prime Minister Benjamin Netanyahu declared a state of war, the first since 1973.

The enduring history of the Jewish people, marked by continuous persecution yet remarkable survival and influence, suggests the presence and involvement of the supernatural. Despite centuries of hardship, the Jewish people have not only endured but have significantly impacted global events.

Interestingly, I (Alex) was filming a video on Jewish history and end-time prophecies the day before the Hamas assault began.[3] The events have led many people to consider afresh the importance of Bible prophecy. In my teaching on that day, I shared five reasons why prophecy is significant:

1. The Bible contains accurate prophecy because only God writes history in advance (and God wrote the Bible).
2. Bible prophecies show God's sovereign reign over world history.

3 Some of this section is adapted from Alex McFarland, "Why Does the Bible Contain Prophecy?," *The Christian Post*, October 12, 2023, https://alexmcfarland.com.

3. Fulfilled prophecies demonstrate God's omniscience and foresight.
4. Fulfilled prophecies prove that the biblical God is the true God and that he reigns in time and in eternity. God "rules and overrules."
5. Fulfilled prophecies should compel every thinking person to bow before the Savior, who alone can offer salvation and amnesty.

Acts 1:7 reminds us that God controls "the times and the seasons" of history. And the historical era we are in is looking forward to the ultimate moment of history: Christ's return.

In this book, we have sought to compile one hundred of the top questions we have heard in our decades of ministry. Some of these questions relate to new technologies that open up new possibilities regarding how the future could unfold.

We are indebted to many Bible prophecy experts who have gone before us, but we felt led to bring to you our unique perspective on these issues in a way we believe the Lord will use to encourage your faith and strengthen your resolve in these trying times.

One enjoyable aspect of this book is the options it provides. You can certainly read from beginning to end, but you can also jump to whatever question stands out to you. Each question and its corresponding answer is designed to stand alone, regardless of whether you have read the rest of the book.

We also encourage you to share this resource with others. Unlike many detailed Christian books that can be overwhelming to receive as gifts, this one is designed with sharing in mind. You can pass your copy along when you're finished or, ideally, purchase additional copies to give to friends and family who are interested in exploring God's Word. For outreach, the book concludes with an "ultimate question" that can help you convey the Bible's message of salvation to others.

Before you start, a couple of notes: We tackle some of the most contentious prophecy issues of our time, and you may not agree with every conclusion, especially on questions where the Bible doesn't provide a definitive answer. We base our responses on Scripture and encourage you to do the same. When interpretations are uncertain, we present various perspectives and allow you to reach your own conclusions as you study.

Second, it's important to recognize the distinction between understanding the truth and living it out. Scripture encourages us not only to know Christ and understand the reasons for our faith but also to apply these beliefs in our lives, impacting both ourselves and those around us. Our aim is not just to provide answers to enhance your knowledge but also to support and inspire your daily walk with Christ.

We also invite you to reach out to us and share how this book has been helpful to you and to ask any further questions you might have. You can contact us through AlexMcFarland.com or email our "Exploring the Word" radio program by email at word@afa.net.

Finally, please know you are in our prayers. We eagerly anticipate connecting with you through God's Word every weekday at AFR.net or on an American Family Radio station near you. May these pages continue to bless you as you seek to better know our Savior and share with others in the days ahead.

SECTION 1

THE LAST DAYS

1. Is Jesus Really Going to Return?

The Bible refers to the return of Jesus on many occasions. For example, in John 14:3 Jesus said, "If I go and prepare a place for you, I will come again and receive you to Myself; that where I am, there you may be also." If the Bible is accurate, and we believe it is 100 percent true, then Jesus is definitely coming back.

Three areas can inform us about Christ's return. They include the predictions of prophecy, Christ's promises, and God's preparations.

The predictions of prophecy include the numerous statements throughout Scripture concerning the return of the Messiah. The Old Testament includes over fifteen hundred passages that refer to the return of the Messiah. For example, Zechariah 12:10 speaks about the pierced Messiah who will appear again. That is why we confidently teach that every Bible-believing Christian believes Jesus will return, even if there is disagreement about the details.

Christ clearly taught that he will return. In Luke 12:40, Jesus said his return would be at an unexpected time: "Therefore you also be ready, for the Son of Man is coming at an hour you do not expect." In Matthew 16:27, Jesus predicted, "The Son of

Man will come in the glory of His Father with His angels, and then He will reward each according to his works."

Even the angels at the ascension of Jesus foretold of Christ's return. Acts 1:11 reveals the angels telling the disciples, "Men of Galilee, why do you stand gazing up into heaven? This same Jesus, who was taken up from you into heaven, will so come in like manner as you saw Him go into heaven."

The passages that prophecy researchers refer to as "rapture references" also point to evidence of Jesus coming at any moment in the future. First Corinthians 15:51–58 describes the Lord providing to believers a new body that will last for eternity. First Thessalonians 4:13–18 also details a future moment when the dead in Christ will rise first, followed by living believers, to be with the Lord forever.

The Bible also notes many preparations God has made for Christ's return. The book of Revelation provides the best description. Its twenty-two chapters outline both the future judgments upon our world and the new heavens and earth that await believers in the end. The description of eternity future was so powerful that the apostle John responded, "Even so, come, Lord Jesus!" (Revelation 22:20).

The details of the end times can be confusing and complicated, but the response to Christ's second coming is clear. The Bible teaches it, Jesus predicted it, and the Lord has prepared a glorious future eternal dwelling for all who have believed in him.

This is why sharing Christ with others today is urgent. We don't know how long we have, whether a day or even an hour. Even if Jesus continues to wait longer to return, it is to allow us to have more time to share him with those around us as we eagerly long for our future time in heaven with our Savior.

2. Some people say that those who obsess over prophecy are "so heavenly-minded that they're of no earthly good." Is it right to focus on prophecy?

It's common to hear Christians, including ministers, say that people who focus on the end times are "so heavenly-minded that they are of no earthly good." What does the Bible teach about focusing on unfulfilled prophecies?

A close look at Scripture reveals quite the opposite. Second Corinthians 4:16–18 says:

> Therefore we do not lose heart. Even though our outward man is perishing, yet the inward man is being renewed day by day. For our light affliction, which is but for a moment, is working for us a far more exceeding and eternal weight of glory, while we do not look at the things which are seen, but at the things which are not seen. For the things which are seen are temporary, but the things which are not seen are eternal.

The apostle Paul was clear: our earthly bodies are fading away. What is eternal is what matters most.

What does it mean to focus on the eternal? First, it includes a deep, daily emphasis on Jesus Christ. He is the one who made us, saves us, and has made a way for us to live with him in heaven.

Second, focusing on the eternal includes an intense study of the Word of God. Scripture is "God-breathed" (2 Timothy 3:16 NIV), serving as an extension of God himself. As we discussed earlier, about 27 percent of the text of the Bible is predictive prophecy, indicating its importance for our lives today.

Third, our eternal focus must include current applications. The saying that we can be of "no earthly good" is true if we spend time studying details about the future without regard for how these teachings apply to our lives today. But God provided prophecies like those found in the book of Revelation to sustain us during difficult moments. Prophecy should also inspire us toward holy living and sharing our faith with those around us.

The prophet Daniel received an overwhelming view of the last days in a vision from God. When he asked about the vision, he was told, "Go your way, Daniel, for the words are closed up and sealed till the time of the end. Many shall be purified, made white, and refined, but the wicked shall do wickedly; and none of the wicked shall understand, but the wise shall understand" (Daniel 12:9–10). God told Daniel that he was to be faithful till the end, knowing that the Lord would fulfill his promises even if Daniel didn't fully understand them.

A proper focus on the prophetic teachings of the Bible will motivate us to live godly lives that serve others with Christ's love. We'll also be sensitive to the need to share the gospel with everyone possible, knowing the consequences that await those who reject his message. Our goal is not only to understand what the Bible teaches about the end times but also to apply these teachings in helping others join us in the future glory that awaits us in the presence of Jesus.

3. What is the Ezekiel 38 battle?

Ezekiel 38:1–17 describes a battle between Israel and many nations that will come against it. God will supernaturally intervene to help Israel win. Many people have asked us questions concerning these verses, including about the identities of the nations and the timing of this battle.

First, the Ezekiel 38 battle has not yet taken place. There has been no united effort by the nations involved against Israel in which God has miraculously defeated these enemies. This means the battle must occur in the future. Some argue that the Ezekiel 38 war could occur at any moment, while others argue that it will take place during the future seven-year tribulation period.

The Bible itself does not specify the timing of the attack and victory. The popular *Left Behind* book and movie portray the battle early in the series, with Israel defeating a military attack. Others suggest that the details in verse 11, particularly that Israel will be living in a time of safety, are an indication that the battle will occur during the first three-and-a-half years of the tribulation before the Antichrist defiles the future Jewish temple. This is most likely, though not certain.

A look at the nations involved also reveals important details. Gog of the land of Magog refers to the land located north of the Black Sea and its leader. This is currently Russia (or at least part of it), indicating that this nation will play a leadership role in a response against Israel during this battle.

Other nations mentioned in the text include Rosh, Meshech, Tubal, Persia, Ethiopia, Libya, Gomer, and Togarmah. The first three nations—Rosh, Meshech, and Tubal—refer to areas around the Black Sea that include Russia and the surrounding lands, perhaps including some of the nations that were part of the former

Soviet Union. Persia refers to modern-day Iran. Ethiopia (or "Cush" in some translations) refers to modern Sudan. Put refers to Libya, while Gomer and Togarmah refer to parts of Turkey. Some also argue that Beth Togarmah is instead Armenia.

The summary of the passage involves a leader from the land of Magog uniting the other nations in a battle against Israel. God supernaturally provides victory, with other nations watching from the outside, including Sheba, Dedan, and others (which likely includes modern Saudi Arabia or the Arabian Peninsula).

Tarshish and its merchants include an unclear reference, with some taking the traditional view of Spain as Tarshish. Others believe it refers to Western nations, including Europe and the Americas.

The battle will show God's power as the ultimate victor. Those who oppose Israel will be defeated as part of the Lord's unfolding future plans. It's important to also note that this battle is different from the battle involving a reference to Gog and Magog in Revelation 20 that addresses an uprising at the end of the millennial kingdom.

4. WHAT DOES THE BIBLE SAY ABOUT RUSSIA IN THE END TIMES?

Many have asked whether Russia is included in the prophecies of the Bible. The nation is often noted among the discussions of Ezekiel 38. Magog, found in Ezekiel 38:1, is a group of nations north of the Black Sea that includes modern Russia. This nation will lead a future coalition of nations in a battle against Israel, according to Ezekiel 38. God promises to supernaturally protect Israel.

Some of the other nations Magog will join in fighting against Israel in the Ezekiel 38 battle include Persia (modern Iran), nations in northern Africa, the Middle East and Central Asia, and Turkey. Many of these countries already oppose the nation of Israel, making it no surprise that such groups would come together against Israel in a future battle.

Revelation 19 also predicts that all nations will join in battle against God and his people at the end of the tribulation period in the battle of Armageddon. This would likely include Russia, though the country is not mentioned by name.

One faulty interpretation of Russia in the Bible, however, occurs when some Bible teachers equate Rosh with Russia. The word translated *Rosh* in Ezekiel 38 is from a Hebrew word meaning "leader" or "head." This refers to the leader of a group rather than to a particular nation. Some have wrongly made the connection between Rosh and Russia due to the similar phonetic sounds between the two names. Others have equated the two names because Rosh is a leader from the area that is likely Russia.

Interestingly, Christianity spread into Russia in the ninth century. Russia has long been known for its Russian Orthodox Church, in many ways operating separately from both the Roman Catholic Church and Protestantism. Christianity was persecuted under the Soviet Union in the twentieth century, though the church ended up growing during this difficult time. A period of revival spread following the fall of the Soviet Union, but growing persecution against Christianity has increased again in recent years.

The Bible has an important history in Russia, especially since what is considered the oldest complete copy of the Hebrew Bible, called the Leningrad Codex, is preserved in St. Petersburg. It has served as the basis for modern Hebrew Bibles used in translating Scripture into English and other languages. The Scriptures were not translated into Russian, however, until the nineteenth century. The Gospels were completed in 1819 with the entire New Testament completed in 1822 and the full Bible in 1876.

The history of Russia includes some significant aspects of Bible prophecy. The nation is predicted to be directly involved in leading a future attack on Israel, though many in Russia continue to live for Christ.

5. IS CHINA MENTIONED IN THE PROPHECIES OF THE BIBLE?

China has the second largest population of any nation and is one of the globe's largest economies. Many have asked us whether China is mentioned in the Bible's end-time prophecies.

The nation of China is not mentioned by name, but some predictions could include this influential country. One example can be found in Revelation 16:12–16. These verses mention "kings from the East" who will march against Israel as part of the battle of Armageddon. These kings could include China along with other influential nations in Asia. Verse 12 explains, "Then the sixth angel poured out his bowl on the great river Euphrates, and its water was dried up, so that the way of the kings from the east might be prepared." Whoever these kings are, they will lead their armies toward Israel for a mighty day of battle.

A second possible example is in Revelation 9. Verse 16 mentions a future army of two hundred million. Currently, this massive number of troops likely could only be met by the military of China. However, this passage might not refer to a literal human army but rather a demonic force. The timing also appears different from the events of Revelation 16.

China will also likely serve as one of the nations led by the Antichrist during the future tribulation period. The Antichrist is predicted to lead the world, including China, though the nation is not directly mentioned.

While some believe China should be mentioned more in the Bible's future predictions, it's also important to remember that the focus of Revelation is on Israel and God's unfolding plan for the Jewish people and Christians. Israel and the nations near it tend to dominate the discussion while other nations, including influential economies like China, the United States, Canada, Australia, and others, are rarely mentioned or are not mentioned at all.

In addition to the negative roles China may play in the end times, Chinese believers will certainly also be among those who worship the Lord in heaven. China may already have the largest population of Christians in history, though persecution makes an accurate number of China's believers difficult to count.

Revelation 7:9–10 clearly predicts:

> After these things I looked, and behold, a great multitude which no one could number, of all nations, tribes, peoples, and tongues, standing before the throne and before the Lamb, clothed with white robes, with palm branches in their hands, and crying out

> with a loud voice, saying, "Salvation belongs to our God who sits on the throne, and to the Lamb!"

Believers from China and every other nation who believe in the Lord Jesus Christ will all worship him together for all eternity. Despite future conflicts on earth, the Lord will unite people from all backgrounds in his presence.

6. WHAT HAPPENS TO AMERICA IN THE END TIMES ACCORDING TO BIBLE PROPHECY?

One of the most common questions we hear concerning Bible prophecy is about America's role in the end times. However, many are unimpressed with our answer, as the Bible does not seem to emphasize our nation's role in the unfolding passages of the last days.

First, the Bible predicts all nations will one day be under the control of a future Antichrist and will join in war against the Lord at the battle of Armageddon (Revelation 19). Yes, even America will one day serve as one of many nations in opposition to God and to Israel.

Second, some see America as one of the nations opposing a future attack on Israel in Ezekiel 38. The reference in Ezekiel 38:13 to "the merchants of Tarshish, and all their young lions" may refer to Western nations, including America. If so, it would fit the common response of many Western nations today to oppose violence against Israel without getting involved to stop it.

Third, many believe the reason America is not emphasized in the end times will be due to many American Christians who will disappear at the rapture. Those who hold a pretribulation view of the rapture see America's role diminished during the tribulation as many in the nation will no longer be on earth during this time.

While this is certainly possible, there is no guarantee America's strength as a world leader will remain until the tribulation. Whether before the tribulation (due to external or internal problems) or during the tribulation (due to persecution or judgment), America and many nations will significantly weaken, leaving them powerless to overcome the Antichrist's leadership.

On the positive side, others see America playing a key role in connection with Israel in the last days. For example, the United States has led in the development of modern Israel and has even moved its embassy to Jerusalem as the capital of the nation. The Abraham Accords, signed in September 2020, have also involved American leadership in normalizing relations between Israel and nations in the Middle East.

Though not directly mentioned, America may serve as part of helping Israel become a land of "unwalled villages" and "peaceful people" (Ezekiel 38:11) in the last days. If so, America will be part of blessing the land as described in Genesis 12:3.

Scripture's focus on Israel and its surrounding nations remains the dominant theme of the end times, but America may have an important role. Individually, we are called to live for the Lord and share him with others as we look forward to the Christ's coming (Hebrews 10:25).

7. IS PSALM 83 ABOUT A FUTURE BATTLE?

Many Bible prophecy teachers discuss the role of Psalm 83. Is this prayer written three thousand years ago a prediction of things to come?

Some suggest that the words of this psalm fit closely with the prophecies in Ezekiel 38–39. For example, many of the same nations are mentioned, and the enemies are united together against Israel. A list of modern equivalents to the names in Psalm 83 include both the nations from Ezekiel and additional areas:

- Tents of Edom: likely southern Jordan
- Ishmaelites: likely Saudi Arabia
- Moab: land currently occupied by Palestinians
- Hagrites: Egypt
- Gebal (or Byblos): likely parts of Lebanon
- Ammon: area currently occupied by Palestinians
- Amalek: the current Sinai area
- Philistia: modern Gaza
- Tyre: southern Lebanon
- Assyria: Syria and/or parts of Iraq

Based on today's volatile events in the Middle East, it is easy to understand why many would associate Psalm 83 and the lands mentioned in it with future battles. However, a close look at the psalm reveals that it likely refers to events in the time of its author, Asaph.

First, Asaph wrote the psalm as a prayer for God to intervene in Israel's trouble happening at the time he wrote it. The same nations surrounding Israel then were at conflict with the

Jewish people, working together in various ways to overtake the people and their land.

Second, the battles noted are too general to refer definitively to future battles. The same people groups fought with Israel before, during, and after the time when Asaph wrote his psalm. To argue that it fits only a future battle overstates the case.

Third, the attempt by some prophecy teachers to connect these ten nations with the ten horns in Revelation 17 is inaccurate. These ten horns likely refer to the revived Roman Empire, not to the nations immediately surrounding Israel. The Antichrist will lead a revived Roman Empire consisting of nations similar to those in the first century that will extend throughout Europe, far beyond the nations listed in Psalm 83.

Psalm 83:1–2 reads, "Do not keep silent, O God! Do not hold Your peace, and do not be still, O God! For behold, Your enemies make a tumult; And those who hate You have lifted up their head." Asaph's focus is on God's response, a plea that fit his time and our time today.

While Psalm 83 may refer to future battles between Israel and its enemies, the song is too vague to interpret as referring only to the future. The more likely interpretation is that it refers to conflicts during the time of Asaph. He was concerned about Israel's enemies uniting to attack them and called on the Lord to answer, just as we are to call to the Lord in our time of need today.

8. Does the Bible Foretell the Destruction of Damascus?

Damascus is the capital of Syria and one of the world's oldest cities. In Isaiah 17, the Bible predicts that this city will be destroyed. Is this a prophecy that has already been fulfilled or will it take place in the future?

The context of this discussion begins in Isaiah 7:7–9. The northern kingdom of Israel, called Ephraim, formed an alliance with Damascus against the southern kingdom of Judah. The Lord delivered a message of reassurance through the prophet Isaiah to predict that Ephraim and Damascus would not succeed and that Judah would win.

The destruction of Damascus is detailed in Isaiah 17:1–3:

> "Behold, Damascus will cease from being a city, and it will be a ruinous heap. The cities of Aroer are forsaken; they will be for flocks which lie down, and no one will make them afraid. The fortress also will cease from Ephraim, the kingdom from Damascus, and the remnant of Syria; they will be as the glory of the children of Israel."

These events would soon take place. King Rezin of Syria and King Pekah of Israel fought against Judah but lost. Rezin was killed, and the city of Damascus was captured by the Assyrians (2 Kings 16:5–9). Prophecy expert Dr. Mark Hitchcock states:

> I believe it makes more sense to hold that Isaiah 17 was fulfilled in the eighth century BC when both Damascus, the capital of Syria, and Samaria, the capital of Israel, were hammered by the Assyrians. In that conquest, both Damascus and Samaria were destroyed,

> just as Isaiah 17 predicts. According to history, Tiglath-pileser III (745–727 BC) pushed vigorously to the west, and in 734 the Assyrians advanced and laid siege to Damascus, which fell two years later in 732.[4]

Some argue that the events described in 2 Kings 16 did not fulfill the prediction of Isaiah 17, however, since Damascus was not completely destroyed. Instead, it is believed that the fulfillment of this prophecy could occur either at an unspecified time in the future or when Christ returns at the second coming.

Nations hostile to Israel will certainly face future judgment. Syria's historical antagonism toward Israel and continued threats suggest that this judgment will be severe. The final destruction of Damascus might occur during Christ's millennial reign from Jerusalem.

While we believe the destruction of Damascus is related to an event that has already taken place in biblical history, there are some good arguments that the predictions may yet point to a future time. This is one prophecy where the exact interpretation of the fall of Damascus related to Bible prophecy is not completely clear, though God offers certainty about his overall place of reigning with his people from a new heavens and new earth (Revelation 21–22).

---

4 Mark Hitchcock, *Middle East Burning: Is the Spreading Unrest a Sign of the End Times?* (Eugene, OR: Harvest House, 2012), 176.

9. What Is the Role of Iran in Bible Prophecy?

In the Bible, Iran is referred to by its historic name, Persia. The nation has a long history in Scripture and a major role in the end times.

The Persian kingdom was well-known to the Jewish people. The kingdom defeated the Babylonians during the time of Daniel, later allowing the Jewish people to return to their homeland, as described by Ezra and Nehemiah. Despite the positive role of the Persian kingdom at the end of the Old Testament period, however, the Bible describes Iran's future role more negatively.

Ezekiel 38–39 is the main section of the Bible that describes Iran's role in the last days. The timing of the battle in this section is not defined but has not yet been fulfilled. Some believe it could take place at any time before the rapture while others place it during the first half of the seven-year tribulation period, when Israel will be in relative peace.

In either scenario, Iran ("Persia") is listed in Ezekiel 38:5 as one of several nations that will join with the leader of Magog (usually identified as Russia) in a battle against Israel. The Lord will provide a supernatural victory, destroying Israel's enemies. The time will also include a massive earthquake in Israel (v. 19).

Verses 21–23 explain some details of this future defeat:

> "I will call for a sword against Gog throughout all My mountains," says the Lord GOD. "Every man's sword will be against his brother. And I will bring him to judgment with pestilence and bloodshed; I will rain down on him, on his troops, and on the many peoples

> who are with him, flooding rain, great hailstones, fire, and brimstone. Thus I will magnify Myself and sanctify Myself, and I will be known in the eyes of many nations. Then they shall know that I am the Lord."

God will rescue his people against Iran at this time, bringing glory to himself in the end. The method of defeat will include causing Israel's enemies to attack one another, along with special events related to weather, such as hail and flooding. Sickness or pestilence will also serve a role in defeating the enemies.

Iran will also certainly be among the nations that oppose God during the battle of Armageddon at the end of the tribulation period. All nations will gather for this battle that will make a united attempt to defeat God's people. Jesus will return in power to defeat these forces as a conquering king.

A look at Iran in our current time reveals a government that views Israel as the Little Satan and America as the Big Satan. In 2024, Iran launched a rocket attack on Israel that was quickly stopped by Israel's defenses. Iran also controls many of the proxy groups at war with Israel, including Hamas and Hezbollah. It will be no surprise to see Iran join with other nations to attack Israel in the last days, but many will be in awe of how God chooses to rescue his people through mighty acts of power.

10. DOES "THE COMING OF CHRIST" SIMPLY REFER TO SOMEONE GETTING BORN AGAIN?

One interesting question we have been asked is whether the idea of the coming of Christ refers to people being saved or born again. This is often due to some ministers urging people to "come to Christ" as a way of encouraging them to come to salvation.

We want to be clear that coming to faith in Christ is a very different action than the future coming of Christ. We are called to believe in the Lord Jesus Christ to be saved. This is the clear message of John 3:16: "God so loved the world that He gave His only begotten Son, that whoever believes in Him should not perish but have everlasting life." Salvation is a gift from the Lord by grace through faith in Jesus (Ephesians 2:8–9).

The coming of Christ, in contrast, refers to the day when Jesus returns. Christians differ in their understanding of the order of future events, but all Bible believers agree that Jesus will come again for his people.

As we mention in response to other questions in this book, the two most likely views are called the pretribulation rapture view and the posttribulation view. The pretribulation view argues that at any moment, Jesus will return for all believers (1 Thessalonians 4:13–18), who will go to heaven with him, and that the seven-year tribulation will follow. Jesus will then come back to earth with all believers at the end of the tribulation at the battle of Armageddon.

The posttribulation view argues that believers will remain on the earth during the tribulation period. In this view, Jesus will come at the end, take believers to be with him, and then defeat his enemies.

This coming of Christ is much different than us coming to Christ. We are called to be saved to live with Jesus for eternity. Jesus will one day return in victory, and then all believers will be with him forever. This second coming is described in several biblical passages. Revelation 19:11–16 provides the most detailed look at this future arrival of Jesus.

> Now I saw heaven opened, and behold, a white horse. And He who sat on him was called Faithful and True, and in righteousness He judges and makes war. His eyes were like a flame of fire, and on His head were many crowns. He had a name written that no one knew except Himself. He was clothed with a robe dipped in blood, and His name is called The Word of God. And the armies in heaven, clothed in fine linen, white and clean, followed Him on white horses. Now out of His mouth goes a sharp sword, that with it He should strike the nations. And He Himself will rule them with a rod of iron. He Himself treads the winepress of the fierceness and wrath of Almighty God. And He has on His robe and on His thigh a name written: KING OF KINGS AND LORD OF LORDS.

Jesus will come someday in the future, but we are called to come to faith in Christ today. We must believe and call others to do so as well, as we do not know when Jesus will choose to return.

SECTION 2

THE SIGNS OF THE END TIMES

11. Will There Be a Global Revival Before the Rapture?

Many pastors and other church leaders teach that a global revival will occur before Jesus returns. Is this true? The basis for this teaching is usually found in Matthew 24:14. Jesus said, "This gospel of the kingdom will be preached in all the world as a witness to all the nations, and then the end will come." Jesus indicates that the gospel will spread worldwide before his return, but the timing is uncertain.

Some argue that this prediction relates to the time before the rapture ahead of the seven-year tribulation. If so, then Jesus' prediction is that the gospel will spread around the world before he returns.

Others understand that Jesus predicted the gospel's spread before his second coming at the end of the tribulation. This interpretation better fits his teachings earlier in Matthew 24, which appear to focus on his return occurring after other events during the tribulation period.

In either case, Jesus does predict the gospel going to all the earth before his final return. The only difference is the timing of this outreach. Regardless of the results we now see in our society, we are called to make disciples of all nations (Matthew 28:18–20). Our goal must be to help every person we possibly can to understand the love of Jesus and receive eternal life (Ephesians 2:8–9; 3:16–19).

Others have looked to Joel 2:28–32 as proof that an outpouring of God's Spirit will bring revival in the last days. Verses 28–29 predict:

> "And it shall come to pass afterward
> That I will pour out My Spirit on all flesh;
> Your sons and your daughters shall prophesy,
> Your old men shall dream dreams,
> Your young men shall see visions.
> And also on My menservants and on My maidservants
> I will pour out My Spirit in those days."

These verses do predict a move of God in the future but were quoted as being fulfilled starting at Pentecost in Acts 2:14–18. Understood in that context, revival has already taken place, beginning with the three thousand people who were baptized in Acts 2:41.

Revelation 14 also foretells that during the tribulation period, one hundred forty-four thousand Jews will boldly share the gospel, leading to a great number of people coming to faith in the Messiah. Revelation 11 also describes two witnesses who will speak of the Messiah. Both examples indicate that many people will come to faith in Jesus during the tribulation, including thousands of Jews.

Even better, Revelation 7:9 describes "a great multitude which no one could number, of all nations, tribes, peoples, and tongues, standing before the throne and before the Lamb." God will save people from every nation and people group who will then be part of our eternal spiritual family.

There may be some dispute about the interpretation of revival ahead of Christ's coming, but there will be a spread of the good news globally as part of God's unfolding plan. We are called to serve as part of fulfilling this great move of our Lord, sharing the gospel both with our neighbors and with the nations as the Lord's promised return nears.

12. HOW CAN I MAKE SURE I AM NOT LEFT BEHIND?

Many end times films and books portray believers disappearing to heaven while nonbelievers are left behind. How can you be certain you are not among those remaining on earth when Jesus calls his followers home?

First, this perspective is based on a pretribulation view of the rapture. This view, as we discuss elsewhere in this book, interprets passages such as 1 Thessalonians 4:13–18 and 1 Corinthians 15:51–58 as describing a time when Jesus comes at any moment to raise the dead in Christ and all living believers to heaven with him before the start of the tribulation period.

Second, the clear difference between who is left behind and who is not is based on faith in Jesus. The "dead in Christ" will be raised first (1 Thessalonians 4:16) and given new spiritual bodies. Those who are alive in Christ will then join them with the Lord. Those who are "caught up" (v. 17) are the people of God who have believed in Jesus by grace through faith.

Verse 18 adds that believers are to "comfort one another with these words." Believers should not fear Christ's coming. We are to look forward to it, longing to be with the Lord and his people forever.

The apostle John clearly had this attitude at the end of Revelation. In Revelation 22:20, he wrote, "Even so, come, Lord Jesus!" When John saw a vision of God's eternal plan for believers, he was excited about what was to come.

The apostle Paul also held this view. In Philippians 1:23, he wrote, "For I am hard-pressed between the two, having a desire to depart and be with Christ, which is far better." He understood that what is ahead of us is far better than anything this world offers.

Jesus taught, "If anyone desires to come after Me, let him deny himself, and take up his cross daily, and follow Me. For whoever desires to save his life will lose it, but whoever loses his life for My sake will save it. For what profit is it to a man if he gains the whole world, and is himself destroyed or lost?" (Luke 9:23–25). We reach heaven by faith in Jesus, but we are also called to live each moment for him, knowing that God has a purpose for us in this world, and that purpose is helping others to grow spiritually.

For believers, this perspective should also challenge us to urgently share Jesus with those who do not know him. We cannot force anyone to believe in him, but we are called to share the gospel with everyone possible. Every believer has a role to play in evangelism as we seek to grow the family of God and help make heaven more crowded.

13. What Are the Seventy Weeks in Daniel?

Daniel includes some of the most amazing—and more difficult—prophecies in the Bible. One of these areas includes the seventy weeks described in the future predictions by the prophet. What are these seventy weeks?

Daniel 9 is the location of this challenging prediction. The angel Gabriel speaks to Daniel about seventy "sevens" for the Jewish people and Jerusalem. The seventy "sevens" are usually understood as weeks, with seventy sevens totaling 490 years.

The prophecy in this chapter then separates the sections into groups of 49 years. Verse 25 says, "Know therefore and understand, that from the going forth of the command to restore and build Jerusalem until Messiah the Prince, there shall be seven weeks and sixty-two weeks; the street shall be built again, and the wall, even in troublesome times."

This prediction indicated that Jerusalem would be restored in less than fifty years. It came true under the king of Persia, when Ezra and Nehemiah led Jews back to the city in a time of revival. The command to rebuild Jerusalem came from King Artaxerxes in about 444 BC.

The next section of 62 "sevens" equals 434 years. Together with the 49 previous years, the total of 483 years would lead to the time of the Messiah. Based on a Jewish calendar of 360-day years, this comes out to 476 years total, or AD 33, the year many historians believe Jesus died on the cross (though some argue for AD 30).

Some scholars have also sought to calculate the exact number of days and argue that the exact day the Scripture was fulfilled occurred when Jesus rode a donkey into Jerusalem as king on Palm Sunday before his rejection and crucifixion. While fascinating if true, it is difficult to say for certain whether the exact days best fit this event or the crucifixion.

Daniel 9:26 then appears to speak about the destruction of Jerusalem shortly after the Messiah comes. The city was destroyed in AD 70.

The final "seven" weeks come following an unknown gap of time and include the seven years of the tribulation period. These years appear to be the same verses described by John in Revelation. During this time, the Antichrist will break a covenant with Israel during the middle of the seven-year tribulation and later face the Messiah's judgment.

The amazing detail of Daniel's prophecy of seventy weeks is often neglected but stands as powerful evidence of God's supernatural ability to predict future events with astounding detail. Just as the Lord has fulfilled many parts of these predictions in the past, we can trust that he will also fulfill the future predictions of a coming seven years of tribulation followed by a time when Christ will return in victory at his second coming.

14. Does the Bible Predict World War III?

The Bible predicts several future wars in its prophecies. Do these predictions fit what would be considered World War III?

In Matthew 24:4–6, Jesus predicted multiple future wars: "Take heed that no one deceives you. For many will come in My name, saying, 'I am the Christ,' and will deceive many. And you will hear of wars and rumors of wars. See that you are not troubled; for all these things must come to pass, but the end is not yet."

War, including the destruction of Jerusalem in AD 70, has sadly been part of our world's long history. In modern history, America, for instance, has endured the Revolutionary War, the War of 1812, the Civil War, two World Wars, the Korean War, the Vietnam War, and wars in Iraq and Afghanistan. These wars do not include the many wars in other nations or the dozens of conflicts worldwide today.

Other than the prediction of the destruction of Jerusalem, these wars and many others were not predicted in the Bible. This means that future wars, including a potential World War III, are still possible.

When people mention World War III, they usually mean a future global war. The Bible does predict conflict during the tribulation. Ezekiel 38 also mentions a future regional war involving Israel and its neighbors that has not yet occurred.

During the future tribulation, which we believe will occur after the rapture, much conflict will arise. There will be persecution against those who do not take the mark of the beast. The two witnesses in Revelation 11 will be killed. A global leader called the Antichrist will accumulate power and punish those who oppose him.

The battle of Armageddon will occur at the end of the seven-year tribulation period when all nations will oppose God in Israel and Jesus will return in victory. Revelation 19:19 predicts,

"And I saw the beast, the kings of the earth, and their armies, gathered together to make war against Him who sat on the horse and against His army."

The Bible is clear about future wars, including a major world conflict at Armageddon. What is unclear is whether any of these wars will be the type of global conflict we would consider World War III. America is not even significantly addressed in Bible prophecy, leaving much unknown about our nation's future role.

What *is* clear is that conflict will remain part of our human experience until Jesus returns. He is the one who will bring peace, defeat evil, and in the end will break the curse of sin. Even at the end of the one-thousand-year millennial kingdom, an uprising will take place one final time, with Jesus defeating Satan and those who oppose God (Revelation 20). Revelation 22:3 says that in the new heavens and earth, "And there shall be no more curse, but the throne of God and of the Lamb shall be in it, and His servants shall serve Him."

15. What Are the Rumors of Wars the Bible Mentions before Christ's Return?

Jesus prophesied that there will be "wars and rumors of war" (Matthew 24:6; Mark 13:7). What are these rumors of war?

In the previous question, we addressed concerns related to wars in the past and future. Rumors of war focuses on talk or discussion of war rather than actual conflict. Jesus predicted that there would be much concern about conflict after he departed from the disciples. Jesus did not want his followers to despair over these rumors. The rest of Matthew 24:6 states, "See that you are not troubled; for all these things must come to pass, but the end is not yet."

Wars and rumors of battles taking place are part of our fallen world. We long for peace but recognize that our broken humanity will include periods of conflict and strife.

Jesus called his disciples to be aware of coming war and, instead of being "troubled" or discouraged over conflict, to remain faithful despite the situations they would face. The same application is true today. When we hear of wars or discussions of potential conflicts close to home or far away, it is easy to become fearful and concerned. Jesus challenges us to instead faithfully endure, knowing that such things are temporary and will one day give way to our eternity in heaven with him.

In today's world, war remains a grim reality. Israel continues to fight for peace and its very existence. For example, on October 7, 2023, Hamas terrorists attacked Israel, killing over twelve hundred people and taking over two hundred fifty people hostage. There was no direct Bible prophecy about this battle, yet it fulfills the pattern of wars in our world until the Lord's coming.

How should we respond to the painful aspects of such wars? In Luke 21:28, Jesus said, "Now when these things begin to happen, look up and lift up your heads, because your redemption draws near." We have confidence in God's plan for eternity despite what happens around us at the moment.

In addition, we are called to pray. Christians are peacemakers, seeking to live in peace whenever possible. Beyond this, we can show acts of kindness to those impacted by war. Some people are also called to military service, law enforcement, or other first responder roles, committing their lives to serving in ways to protect the safety of others.

When we look ahead to the end of God's ultimate plan, we discover an end to death and sorrow in the new heavens and earth. Revelation 21:3–4 reminds us, "God Himself will be with them and be their God. And God will wipe away every tear from their eyes; there shall be no more death, nor sorrow, nor crying. There shall be no more pain, for the former things have passed away." God will make all things new (v. 5) and will remove the curse of sin (22:3).

In 1 Thessalonians 4:18, Paul also told believers to be encouraged at the future rapture of believers. We are not without hope, and we can look forward to our future home, which will be free from war and conflict.

16. What Does It Mean That Jesus Will Come Like a Thief in the Night?

In 1 Thessalonians 5:2, Paul wrote, "For you yourselves know perfectly that the day of the Lord so comes as a thief in the night." What does this mean and how should these words apply to our lives?

The example Paul used was well-known to his readers. A person robbing a home usually comes at night and without warning. Paul compared this criminal action with the surprising nature of Christ's return at his second coming. Jesus will come unexpectedly, catching many people off guard and unprepared.

In verse 3, Paul added that people will be declaring, "Peace and safety!" These words connect with the message of the future Antichrist who will confirm a seven-year peace agreement during the tribulation period. As people expect peace, disaster will come upon them, both in the judgments unfolding in Revelation and when Jesus returns to defeat his enemies at Armageddon (Revelation 19).

The application of this message is not only for those in the future. Paul explained that Christians are to live aware of Christ's coming now. First Thessalonians 5:6–8 teaches: "Therefore let us not sleep, as others do, but let us watch and be sober. For those who sleep, sleep at night, and those who get drunk are drunk at night. But let us who are of the day be sober, putting on the breastplate of faith and love, and as a helmet the hope of salvation." Verse 11 adds, "Therefore comfort each other and edify one another, just as you also are doing."

The three themes of faith, hope, and love also reflect the applications Paul provided in 1 Corinthians 13, adding that the greatest of these is love. Our response to Christ's return is not fear or doubt but rather love for God and others expressed through acts of faith and an anticipation of hope for what he has done and will do in the future.

Jesus also mentioned the idea of a thief coming at night in Matthew 24:43–44: "But know this, that if the master of the house had known what hour the thief would come, he would have watched and not allowed his house to be broken into. Therefore you also be ready, for the Son of Man is coming at an hour you do not expect."

In these verses, Jesus emphasized readiness. Believers should be motivated to holy living when we consider Christ's return.

In 2 Peter 3:10, we read similar words: "But the day of the Lord will come as a thief in the night, in which the heavens will pass away with a great noise, and the elements will melt with fervent heat; both the earth and the works that are in it will be burned up." Peter again emphasizes the sudden coming of Jesus and a time when the new heavens and earth will transform our world, making all things new.

As discussed elsewhere, there is some dispute among Bible teachers over the timing of Christ's coming. We hold the view that Jesus' rapture coming could be at any time (1 Thessalonians 4:13–18), followed by the seven-year tribulation and then the return of Jesus at his second coming. Others combine these two events, believing Jesus will return for his people after the tribulation and then defeat his enemies at Armageddon in one event.

In either case, the call to be prepared for Christ's any-moment coming applies. Just as a thief arrives suddenly and without warning, Jesus will make a sudden appearance, which challenges us to live every moment of every day to its fullest, honoring him with our lives and sharing his love with others.

17. What Does the Bible Mean That Elijah Must Return Before the End Times?

The Old Testament's final chapter includes a mysterious prediction that the prophet Elijah will return before the day of the Lord (Malachi 4:5–6). What do these words mean?

The Jewish teachers in the time of Jesus took the words literally, looking forward to a time when Elijah would come again. When John the Baptist began growing in popularity through his revival teaching and baptisms, the religious leaders even asked him if he was Elijah.

Jesus soon revealed that these Jewish leaders were on the right track. In Matthew 11:13–14, he stated, "For all the prophets and the law prophesied until John. And if you are willing to receive it, he is Elijah who is to come." John the Baptist was the fulfillment of Malachi's prophecy, serving as a messenger ahead of the Messiah's coming.

The disciples asked Jesus about this prophecy again in Matthew 17:10–13. The disciples asked:

> "Why then do the scribes say that Elijah must come first?"
>
> Jesus answered and said to them, "Indeed, Elijah is coming first and will restore all things. But I say to you that Elijah has come already, and they did not know him but did to him whatever they wished. Likewise the Son of Man is also about to suffer at their hands." Then the disciples understood that He spoke to them of John the Baptist.

The phrase "whatever they wish" referred to the persecution and death of John the Baptist. The Tetrarch Herod Antipas arrested him, and he was later beheaded by Herod's executioner (14:1–12). Herod arrested John because he spoke out against Herod's marriage to Herodias as unlawful. She had previously been the wife of Herod's brother.

The daughter of Herodias later danced during Herod's birthday party. Herod was so pleased that he offered her anything she wanted as a gift. After consulting her mother, the young woman asked for John the Baptist's head on a platter. Herod reluctantly agreed, ending the life of the young spiritual leader.

Interestingly, John the Baptist was also a relative of Jesus. Luke's Gospel begins with the longest account of how John's parents conceived him in their old age. Mary the mother of Jesus was a relative of John's mother, Elizabeth. Mary traveled to Elizabeth's home and stayed with her during the time when both of them were pregnant. John was approximately six months older than Jesus (Luke 1).

Some have argued that John the Baptist was not the fulfillment of the prophecy of Elijah because he told the religious leaders he was not (John 1:21). However, the likely explanation is that John did not view himself in this way. Jesus was the one who taught that John specifically fulfilled the prediction of Malachi 4.

The life of John the Baptist should inspire us to live for God in our own lives. He sacrificed many earthly benefits to teach God's ways and lead many to repentance. We are likewise called to give up our personal preferences to live for the Lord and to invest our lives in sharing Christ with those around us.

SECTION 3

THE ROLE OF ISRAEL AND BIBLE PROPHECY

18. WHAT WILL ISRAEL'S ROLE BE IN THE LAST DAYS?

Israel often appears in the Bible's prophecies. What is the role of this important nation in the last days?

Scripture provides many ways in which Israel will be influential in the last days. First, Israel will be a nation, something that was not true from AD 70 until 1948. The reestablishment of modern Israel is a testimony that God fulfills his promises and has a literal plan for Israel in the future.

Second, the Bible predicts a return of many Jews to Israel in the end times. Ezekiel 36:24 predicts, "For I will take you from among the nations, gather you out of all countries, and bring you into your own land." Isaiah 43:6 adds, "Bring My sons from afar, and My daughters from the ends of the earth." Millions of Jews have returned from around the world to the Jewish homeland in Israel, bringing these words to life in a vivid way in our times.

Third, the future tribulation includes the Antichrist making a covenant of peace with Israel that will be broken after three and a half years. Daniel 9:27 predicts concerning Israel, "Then he shall confirm a covenant with many for one week; but in the middle of the week He shall bring an end to sacrifice and offering." The weeks in this context refer to seven-year periods of time.

Fourth, Israel will one day recognize Jesus as the Messiah. Zechariah 12:10 predicts, "And I will pour on the house of David and on the inhabitants of Jerusalem the Spirit of grace and supplication; then they will look on Me whom they pierced. Yes, they will mourn for Him as one mourns for his only son, and grieve for Him as one grieves for a firstborn."

Fifth, many see the revival of the Hebrew language in Israel as a fulfillment of Bible prophecy. Zephaniah 3:9 says, "For then I will restore to the peoples a pure language, that they all may call on the name of the Lord, to serve Him with one accord." The use of Hebrew died out to near extinction until the late nineteenth century. When Israel was restored as a nation, Hebrew became one of its official languages and is now spoken by millions of people.

Other predictions from Ezekiel 38 include Israel winning a future battle against its enemies and Jesus ruling from Israel during the millennial kingdom. Ultimately, God will create a new heavens and earth, including a New Jerusalem that will surpass all cities in greatness (Revelation 21).

Israel is already fulfilling some of the Bible's predictions. However, this important nation will continue to play a vital role in the unfolding plan of God and the complete fulfillment of his promises to Abraham and the Jewish people.

19. WHY IS MODERN ISRAEL CONSIDERED A MAJOR SIGN OF THE END TIMES?

Many Bible teachers consider the rebirth of Israel as a nation as a "super sign" of the end times. Why is the return of this historic nation to its homeland so important in Bible prophecy?

The primary reason Israel's rebirth is considered important is because many predictions in Revelation and other prophetic books of the Bible discuss Israel as a nation. In other words, before Israel was a nation again, many of the predictions in Bible prophecy would have been difficult to see coming to fulfillment. Now that it is a nation again, it is easier to see how God could bring forth many of the predictions found in Scripture concerning the last days.

A second reason why Israel's rebirth is important is the Bible's predictions of a future Jewish temple in Jerusalem. Daniel 9:24–27 foretells that the Antichrist will desecrate the Jewish temple. Jesus confirmed this prediction in Matthew 24:15.

Revelation reveals that the Antichrist will break his covenant with Israel at the midpoint of the tribulation. This will take place in the Jewish temple, something that does not exist today except for the remaining Western Wall in Jerusalem.

Many prophecy teachers believe that between the rapture and the midpoint of the tribulation, a new Jewish temple will be rebuilt as part of the Antichrist's promise of peace. In Israel, an organization called the Temple Institute has already established detailed plans to rebuild a temple in the future. In addition to the temple, the furnishings, vessels, and other instruments needed for ritual sacrifices and worship have been created.

For now, construction on the Temple Mount remains blocked due to tensions between Jews and Muslims. The Al-Aqsa Mosque, which now stands on the Temple Mount site, compounds these tensions. Some argue that the Temple Mount is the most volatile piece of real estate on the planet due to the many conflicts over who should control the location.

While many details remain a mystery, the reestablishment of modern Israel following World War II marked a major change, providing a literal nation and land where the Bible's prophecies could be fulfilled. The change also led to a new understanding of many of the Bible's predictions in a more literal manner rather than seeking to interpret references to Israel symbolically.

The very land Abraham was promised and where Jesus and his followers walked is now a Jewish homeland once again. Despite political differences and concerns in this land today, the emergence of modern Israel provides strong testimony that God fulfills his promises and continues to have a plan for Israel, the Jewish people, and for the many Bible predictions yet to unfold.

20. Will the Generation That Saw Israel Reborn Be Alive to See the Rapture?

In Matthew 24:34, Jesus said, "Assuredly, I say to you, this generation will by no means pass away till all these things take place." Does this mean that the generation alive when Israel became a nation again in 1948 will be the people who see the rapture?

If so, the rapture would already have taken place. It has been over seventy-five years since Israel became a modern nation, a period that is longer than what is considered a generation.

The context of the passage emphasizes that the generation living when the signs Jesus mentioned begin to happen will see them fulfilled. In other words, Jesus seems to speak about the future seven-year tribulation. Once the events begin to unfold, those alive will see the remaining predictions occur within a short time.

Three major predictions appear in Matthew 24 that have not yet occurred. First, Jesus spoke of the abomination of desolation. This is a reference to the future Antichrist desecrating the Jewish temple at the midpoint of the tribulation period.

Second, Jesus referred to the "great tribulation." This period is a shorter time within the larger tribulation, during which the most intense consequences will fall upon the earth.

Third, Jesus spoke of signs in the heavens. These signs likely relate to actions described in Revelation that include changes with the sun, moon, and stars.

Other interpreters view the generation passage as referring to Jesus' prediction of the destruction of Jerusalem in AD 70. While this is possible, some of the predictions in Matthew 24 strongly indicate a future time, when judgment will be far worse than the burning of one city.

Still others suggest that the "generation" refers to a group of people: namely, the Jews. In this understanding, the Jewish people will not pass away until the signs Jesus predicted are fulfilled. The conclusion is true, but the interpretation appears to be more specific than referring to the Jewish people.

Overall, the context of Matthew 24 indicates that the future tribulation will unfold quickly. Revelation defines this time of judgment as a seven-year tribulation. Those who are alive at that time will see all of these prophecies unfold quickly many generations after Jesus predicted the events.

21. Will All Israel Be Saved in the End Times?

Romans 11:26 says, "All Israel will be saved." Does this mean all Jewish people will believe in Jesus as Messiah someday?

Some have taken the view that Israel has been replaced by the church and that the verse applies to Christians (also known as "replacement theology"). However, this interpretation takes this verse out of context. Paul was addressing the literal Jewish people of Israel.

The context of Romans 11 clearly distinguishes the natural branches as Jews while the wild branches are gentiles or non-Jews. The Jews would be cut off while gentiles are grafted in, indicating salvation through Jesus as the Messiah. Verse 28 adds, "Concerning the gospel they are enemies for your sake, but concerning the election they are beloved for the sake of the fathers." The Jews were opposed to gentile Christians at the time but were still chosen or elected by God.

Other passages foretell that many Jews will one day believe in the Messiah. Today, reportedly less than one percent of Israeli Jews believe in Jesus as the Messiah (also known as Messianic Jews). Worldwide, the percentage of Jews who are believers in Jesus is about 2.2 percent. In the future, many others will believe.

During the tribulation, one hundred forty-four thousand Jews will share the gospel with others, indicating at least hundreds of thousands of Jews who will believe in Jesus as the Messiah (Revelation 14). Those who believe during this time will endure much persecution.

Zechariah 12:10 offers more insight into the future response to Jesus from the Jewish people: "And I will pour on the house of David and on the inhabitants of Jerusalem the Spirit of grace and supplication; then they will look on Me whom they pierced. Yes, they will mourn for Him as one mourns for his only son, and grieve for Him as one grieves for a firstborn."

Many will turn to the Messiah in the last days, including those among the Jewish people. Even today, missionaries and other groups seek to tell the good news of the Messiah to Jews, and there are reports of many Jewish people trusting in the Lord. However, a future time is coming when a massive number of Jews will turn to the Messiah, fulfilling God's promises of Israel being saved.

Others see this fulfillment also unfolding during the future thousand-year millennial kingdom. When Jesus returns at the battle of Armageddon (Revelation 19), he will then reign from his throne in Jerusalem. In this sense, all Israel will be saved too, with Christ's followers being with him until God defeats his enemies' final rebellion and establishes a new heavens and new earth.

22. What Is the "Time of Jacob's Trouble"?

The time of Jacob's trouble is often mentioned in Bible prophecy. What is it, and what does it mean concerning the end times?

The origin of the phrase is found in Jeremiah 30:7: "Alas! For that day is great, so that none is like it; and it is the time of Jacob's trouble, but he shall be saved out of it." The context of Jeremiah 30 is often connected with the events of the seven-year tribulation period, making it an important part of yet unfulfilled Bible prophecy.

There are several reasons why many interpreters connect the time of Jacob's trouble with the tribulation. First, the context indicates a time of blessing that will come after this trouble. For example, verse 11 adds, "'For I am with you,' says the Lord, 'to save you; though I make a full end of all nations where I have scattered you, yet I will not make a complete end of you. But I will correct you in justice, and will not let you go altogether unpunished.'" Verse 7 adds that there will be no other time like this time.

Since the tribulation marks the most violent upheaval prior to Christ's return, it makes the most sense to connect this time with this future period. The nations against Israel will also be defeated at this time, a likely reference to Christ's coming to defeat his enemies at the battle of Armageddon (Revelation 19) at the end of the tribulation.

The events also seem to parallel the predictions described by Jesus in Matthew 24. Verse 21 describes this period as one of "great tribulation, such as has not been since the beginning of the world until this time, no, nor ever shall be." It will also be a time of "wars and rumors of wars" (v. 6).

During this tribulation period, the Jewish temple will be reconstructed and later defiled. The Antichrist will break a treaty, proclaim himself as the supreme ruler, and demand to be worshiped. He will impose a system where everyone must receive a mark to buy or sell. There will be widespread conflict and famine, causing Jews to flee Jerusalem and seek refuge in the mountains.

Despite these troubles, the Lord will keep his promises. He will guard his people and will also return in triumph (Revelation 19:11–21). After his victory, the Messiah will reign in peace from Jerusalem for one thousand years (20:1–6). Following a final rebellion led by Satan, the Lord will conquer his foes, carry out his ultimate judgment, and create a new heaven, a new earth, and a New Jerusalem, where he will reside with his people forever (21:1–22).

These prophecies shared in Revelation increase our understanding of the period that Jeremiah calls "the time of Jacob's trouble." With the arrival of Jesus Christ as the Messiah, some of Jeremiah's prophecies have already been fulfilled. When he comes again, the remaining aspects will be completed, and God's people will dwell with him forever.

SECTION 4

VIEWS OF THE RAPTURE

23. WAS THE RAPTURE "INVENTED" IN MODERN TIMES AND THUS NOT BIBLICAL?

Some people have told us that they have been taught that the rapture is a modern teaching. Is this true? Even online sources like Wikipedia claim that the rapture is not found in historic Christianity. A close look at the biblical and historical teachings of the rapture shows that it is both a biblical and a historical teaching of the church.

The rapture is generally defined as the time when Jesus comes for his believers at any moment (1 Corinthians 15:51–58; 1 Thessalonians 4:13–18). The rapture is followed by the seven-year tribulation described in Revelation and then Christ's second coming at the battle of Armageddon (Revelation 19).

This view became popularized in the 1800s under the teaching of British minister John Nelson Darby. He helped found the Plymouth Brethren Church and published a booklet called *The Nature and Unity of the Church of Christ.* Its views focused on a distinction between Israel and the church, contrasting the view of replacement theology that teaches that the church has replaced Israel. His booklet also emphasized Jesus returning before the tribulation and then returning to earth at the second coming.

His teachings were later expanded and popularized in the Scofield Study Bible. This Bible fueled the dispensational views of the twentieth century that influenced the Bible Conference movement, Bible churches, and dispensational schools like Dallas Theological Seminary.

Despite the popularity of these views in the past two hundred years, they have been held throughout church history. Professor and prophecy expert Dr. Thomas Ice discusses the history of the rapture view in an article, noting, "Expressions of imminency abound in the Apostolic Fathers. Clement of Rome, Ignatius of Antioch, *The Didache, The Epistle of Barnabas*, and *The Shepherd of Hermas* all speak of imminency. Furthermore, *The Shepherd of Hermas* speaks of the pretribulational concept of escaping the tribulation."[5]

His paper also notes examples found throughout the Middle Ages and among some writers during the Protestant Reformation. Even those Reformers who rejected the view showed that it was discussed and held by others during their time.

The last two centuries have seen a resurgence in interest in Bible prophecy as vast changes have impacted our world. It should not surprise us that more people look to Scripture for information on the details of the last days, including the rapture and its relationship to the tribulation period. All believers

---

5 Thomas D. Ice, "A Brief History of the Rapture," Liberty University, May 2009, *Article Archives* 4, https://digitalcommons.liberty.edu/pretrib_arch/4.

look forward to Jesus coming again, despite differences in the timing. No matter one's particular view on particular events, the primary focus for all Christians must remain on living for God, living by his Spirit, and sharing Christ with others.

On the Origins of End-Time Belief Systems

It is sometimes asserted that belief in the rapture of the church and the triumphant return of Christ are mere recent developments, and such doctrines are therefore not scripturally valid. Liberal theologians often attribute (in a pejorative sense) current understandings of end-time events to a certain John N. Darby (1800–1882). Those who may believe in the eventual return of Christ—but who do not believe that Christians will be "caught up to meet the Lord in the air"—often assert that Darby "invented" the rapture. Quite often, callers to our radio program will say, "My pastor says that belief in the rapture didn't exist prior to the 1800s."

Who Was John Nelson Darby?

John Darby was a lawyer who became a leader in the church of Ireland and an ordained clergyman of the Church of England. Around 1831, Darby organized Christian groups in the Dublin area devoted to the study of God's Word and living out Christian principles. Darby wrote forty volumes of six hundred pages each, more than twenty-four thousand pages of content. He researched and wrote on theology, philosophy, church history, and even completed a translation of the Bible from the original languages.

The views of popular Christian authors such as Tim LaHaye (author of the *Left Behind* series), Charles Ryrie, H. L. Willmington, John F. Walvoord, Billy Graham, David Jeremiah, Jonathan Cahn, and others are regularly dismissed as being so-called variations of nineteenth-century Darbyism.

Such criticisms are sometimes leveled by theological liberals, who reject belief in biblical authority or Christ's return in any form. Others are simply parroting critiques of teachings that take the prophetic passages of Scripture literally. Those who oppose conservative eschatology often do so because of philosophical bias, which invariably includes a rejection of the miraculous. Such metaphysical bias requires a rejection of both prophecy and scriptural inerrancy.

Theological labels aside, many recognize that anything less than a futurist analysis of Revelation 4–22 jeopardizes many other biblical realities. A non-literal interpretation of the rapture or millennium implies a non-literal understanding of other key scriptural truths, such as the physical resurrection of Christ or the first resurrection of believers, for example. We (the authors) hold to a futurist interpretation of Revelation chapters 4–22.

WAS JOHN'S REVELATION PROPHECY? HISTORY? SOCIOLOGY?

The content of John's Revelation is, admittedly, complex. It is doubtful that in all of church history any single scholar has accurately grasped *everything* in the Bible's final book. However, there is much in the book that is forthrightly stated and can be plainly understood.

Related to the subject of whether John Darby originated a premillennial interpretation of key prophetic passages is the general topic of hermeneutics. We (the authors) believe that the words of the book of Revelation should be taken at face value. After all, words do have meanings, and combinations of words convey meaning. Words are vehicles that can convey objective meaning and therefore truth.

Even those who dismiss Revelation as allegory and symbolic use words in a literal (objective) sense to assert that Revelation is not objective. They use rational argumentation (in a forensic sense) to try and dissuade anyone from viewing Revelation as propositional or as depicting objective truth.

We believe that Revelation 4–22 should be understood in a future sense. None of the events after chapter 3 have occurred as of yet. The events of the book have a built-in chronological order. Chapters 4 and following do exhibit a clear, sequential order. Acceptance of the book in a literal, sequential, chronological manner—we believe— makes the most sense. Now, back to our response to the dismissal of premillennialism as nothing but Darbyism.

THE GENETIC FALLACY

The question is not "Where did 'such and such' teaching originate?" The question should be "Is this or that teaching *true*?" Premillennialism, broadly speaking, concludes that biblical prophecy sets forth a future that will play out as follows:

> Rapture > tribulation > Armageddon > Christ's return > a one-thousand-year millennium > new heavens and earth

John Nelson Darby was certainly not the first Christian leader to set forth an understanding of the end times that included a premillennial return of Christ. Other ancient Christian leaders teaching a similar eschatology included Clement of Rome (AD 30–95), Polycarp (70–155), Ignatius (35–107), Papius (ca. 60–130), Justin Martyr (100–164), Irenaeus (ca. 130–200), Tertullian (160–240), Cyprian (200–258), and Lactanitus (240–320). Renowned scholar Augustine (354–430) initially held to a premillennial view but later changed his position.

Disagreements do occur over the minute points of biblical eschatology, and equally good believers may embrace divergent points of view on various subjects. This is to be expected given the fact that we live in a fallen world and the human intellect is limited. While God's revelation is perfect, our comprehension of it is not.

Still, the points of orthodoxy on which Christians agree is that Christ will return, will judge the world in righteousness, and will usher in his eternal kingdom. "Let us then wait for the Kingdom of God from hour to hour in love and righteousness, seeing that we know not the day of the appearing of God" (Clement of Rome).

---

24. What Does It Mean That the Rapture Is Imminent?

What does it mean that the rapture is imminent? The word *imminent* means able to happen at any moment. The Bible teaches that Jesus will fulfill his promise to come at an unspecified future time to take believers to be with him forever.

In John 14:2–4, Jesus taught, "In My Father's house are many mansions; if it were not so, I would have told you. I go to prepare a place for you. And if I go and prepare a place for you, I will come again and receive you to Myself; that where I am, there you may be also. And where I go you know, and the way you know." He promised to come back at a future moment to take his followers into his eternal presence.

In 1 Corinthians 15:51–52, Paul describes what we believe is a key passage describing the rapture: "Behold, I tell you a mystery: We shall not all sleep, but we shall all be changed—in a moment, in the twinkling of an eye, at the last trumpet. For the trumpet will sound, and the dead will be raised incorruptible, and we shall be changed." He emphasizes the events taking place in a single moment. The "twinkling of an eye" likely refers to something that occurs in less than a second.

Some argue that this passage could refer to Jesus returning at the end of the tribulation. While possible, the details appear to discuss believers being raised to life to join the Lord in heaven in a way that closely fits 1 Thessalonians 4:13–18. We agree with others who hold a pretribulation view that see Jesus coming at any moment to take believers to be with him and later returning with raptured believers at the end of the tribulation period. We discuss some of these differences further in the next question.

In 1 Thessalonians 4:13–18, Paul gives some of the details regarding the order of events at the rapture. First, Jesus will descend from heaven with a shout (v. 16). There will also be a voice of an archangel with a trumpet.

Second, the dead in Christ will rise first. This teaching indicates that the bodies of believers will be transformed into new heavenly bodies in the presence of the Lord. The souls of believers who have passed away will be reconnected with a new heavenly body at the rapture.

Third, living believers will go up to the Lord, transformed into eternal bodies, to be with him forever. Paul ends the passage by telling his readers to encourage one another with these words (v. 18). This was not a scary or discouraging teaching but rather a reason to rejoice as believers look forward to being with the Lord and his people forever.

The emphasis on the imminent rapture holds great importance for all believers but also strengthens the view of the pretribulation rapture. Other views hold that Jesus returns at some point during or at the end of the seven-year tribulation, a perspective that does not appear to fit believers looking forward to Christ's coming at any moment.

Many Bible passages emphasize our anticipation of Christ's coming. For example, 1 John 3:2–3 says, "Beloved, now we are children of God; and it has not yet been revealed what we shall be, but we know that when He is revealed, we shall be like Him, for we shall see Him as He is. And everyone who has this hope in Him purifies himself, just as He is pure." The imminent rapture should fill us with joy and hope as we look forward to his coming and our future eternity with him.

25. What Are the Differences Between the Rapture and the Second Coming?

Do the rapture and the second coming of Jesus refer to one event or two? A close look at the Bible shows that there are significant differences between these two future events that point to them being separate rather than the same.

Various Bible teachers have highlighted a dozen or more key distinctions between these two events. Before the second coming of Christ, several prophecies must be fulfilled, including the return of Israel as a nation, the rebuilding of the temple in Jerusalem, and the events of the tribulation as outlined in Revelation. However, the rapture of the church does not require any specific prophecies to be fulfilled. The rapture could occur at any moment, with believers being caught up to meet the Lord in the air (1 Thessalonians 4:16–17).

During the rapture, Christ's feet will not touch the earth; instead, he will meet believers "in the air" (v. 17). In contrast, at the second coming, Christ's feet will touch the earth, leading to dramatic geographical changes.

For instance, Zechariah 14:4 describes how the Mount of Olives will split into two parts when Jesus returns: "In that day His feet will stand on the Mount of Olives, which faces Jerusalem on the east. And the Mount of Olives shall be split in two, from east to west, making a very large valley; half of the mountain shall move toward the north and half of it toward the south."

At the rapture, Jesus will return to heaven with his believers whereas at the second coming, he will come back to earth with his followers to establish his kingdom. The rapture is a mystery not revealed in the Old Testament, and it pertains solely to the church, while the second coming is extensively foretold in the Old Testament as part of God's plan for Israel, the church, and the world.

Following the rapture, believers will face judgment at the judgment seat of Christ (2 Corinthians 5:10), determining their rewards in heaven. After the second coming, unbelievers will be judged at the great white throne judgment (Revelation 20:11–15), which is the final judgment for all unbelievers.

There will be no physical changes to the earth after the rapture, but the second coming will bring about a partial renovation of the planet as part of the curse is lifted. In addition, following the rapture, Satan will be active on earth for seven years while after the second coming, he will be bound for one thousand years.

The rapture will occur instantly, "in the twinkling of an eye" (1 Corinthians 15:52), while the second coming will conclude seven years of global conflict involving millions. At the rapture, only believers will see Christ. In contrast, at the second coming, unbelievers will see him whom they have pierced

(Zechariah 12:10), and every knee will bow, and every tongue will confess that Jesus Christ is Lord to the glory of God the Father (Philippians 2:10–11).

Other differences also exist, but this list offers substantial biblical evidence that the rapture and second coming are two unique events in God's prophetic timeline important for our study today.

26. What Does It Mean That "No One Knows the Day nor the Hour of Christ's Return"?

Jesus taught in Mark 13:32 that no one knows the day or hour of Christ's return. What does this mean?

Day and hour refer to general periods, but the return of Jesus is a specific event. Jesus appears to prepare his followers to live for him without knowing when his coming will occur. His disciples expected Jesus to fulfill the role of the Messiah who would rule from Jerusalem right away. They did not understand that he would suffer, die, rise from the dead, and ascend to heaven before returning in the future.

In this passage, Jesus explicitly stated that he will not provide any specific details about the timing of his return. He refrained from suggesting a precise date or time, asserting that no one knows when it will happen. This "no one" includes the angels in heaven, who, as Jesus had just mentioned, will play a significant role in his return.

Even Jesus said he does not know the exact time. Some interpret this as a challenge to his divinity, but it aligns with his role within the Trinity and his earthly ministry. As both fully human and fully divine, Jesus experienced growth in both physical and intellectual capacities after his birth (Luke 2:52), yet he remained morally perfect (Hebrews 4:15) and possessed divine knowledge as the Son of God (John 16:30).

Ultimately, only God the Father knows the precise moment of Christ's second coming. Jesus indicates that the Son will await the Father's command to return. This submission is part of the divine mystery of Jesus, as Paul outlines in Philippians 2:6–7 that Jesus, "being in the form of God, did not consider it robbery to be equal with God, but made Himself of no reputation, taking the form of a bondservant, and coming in the likeness of men."

Those who have called for Christ's coming at a specific time in history have been proven as fools or false teachers. To pursue an exact time is contrary to God's clear teachings. His coming is not based on some teacher's specific prediction or an ancient calendar.

Attempting to pinpoint the exact moment of Christ's return is a worthless pursuit. It remains unknown. Any individual or group that claims to know a specific date for Christ's return is misleading. No one can know more about the timing than this: when the foretold signs begin to manifest (Matthew 24:15, 29–30), it will be clear that the end is imminent. Until then, God's plan for the future remains a mystery.

Jesus is near, standing at the door, where he could come at any moment (Matthew 24:33). This perspective is designed to motivate us to live every moment for the Lord, living ready and alert in a world in need of his grace.

27. WHO WILL GO TO BE WITH JESUS AT THE RAPTURE?

In addition to debate concerning views of the rapture, there is also some question about the people who will go to heaven at this time. Many of these questions focus on those who are young, those unable to understand salvation, or those who have never heard the gospel.

The Bible's two main passages addressing the rapture focus on believers in Christ. In 1 Thessalonians 4:13–18, the dead in Christ will rise first and then living believers will be caught up with the Lord. There is no direct mention of others, leaving unanswered details in some areas.

Many have argued that young children will be taken to heaven at the rapture. This is due to an understanding that the Bible indicates young children who pass away go to heaven. For example, when David's infant son died, he took comfort that he would go to be with him, referring to heaven (2 Samuel 12:23).

When it comes to the rapture, however, this application is uncertain. Children will likely go to heaven during the rapture, and this is our view. However, this is not specifically stated. Some have concluded that it is at least possible that unbelieving children would be left on earth to continue life and later choose whether to believe.

A similar discussion applies to those unable to believe, including individuals with mental developmental issues who may not be able to understand the gospel message. We would argue the same idea applies as with young children, though the Bible does not specifically address this area.

What about those who have never heard the gospel? They will not be taken to heaven in the rapture. Multitudes of people will remain on the earth who have not believed. It appears clear that some of these individuals will be people who have not heard about Jesus. Hope will remain, however, as large numbers of people will still believe in Jesus during the tribulation period.

Believers during the tribulation will face more persecution than Christians do today, but many who reject the gospel or have not even heard about Jesus before the rapture will turn to faith in Jesus during this difficult time, revealing God's grace even during this challenging time in the future.

In the end, we know that God is perfect and just in all his ways. We can trust that he will perfectly determine who should be with him at the rapture and who will not. Our calling is to believe in him, live for him, and share him with others as we look forward to his coming.

28. What Is the Most Likely Outline of the End Times?

Many timelines have been presented regarding the end times. The two most common outlines are based on the pretribulation rapture and the posttribulation rapture. Some have also developed timelines based on a midtribulation view. According to our understanding of Scripture, the pretribulation view best accounts for the details regarding unfulfilled prophecy.

In this understanding, the outline of events begins with the next imminent event, the rapture of believers. Both 1 Corinthians 15:51–58 and 1 Thessalonians 4:13–18 describe

Christ raising dead believers and then living believers to be in his presence forever. John 14:1–3 also describes Jesus returning for his believers in what could be considered a rapture passage.

Following this time, the Antichrist will come to power and either sign or confirm a seven-year covenant with Israel (Daniel 9:27). A growing number of troubles will come upon the world as defined in the seven seal, trumpet, and bowl judgments of Revelation 6–18.

At the midpoint of these seven years, the Antichrist will break his agreement with Israel and defile the temple in the abomination of desolation (Daniel 9:27). He will require all people to worship him, enforcing the mark of the beast as a requirement for buying or selling (Revelation 13).

The second half of the tribulation is referred to as the great tribulation. It is also described as the time of Jacob's trouble and will include further outpourings of God's wrath on the earth.

The end of the seven-year tribulation will include both a final attack by the Antichrist against Jerusalem and the battle of Armageddon. Jesus will return with his people and angelic forces to destroy his enemies, casting them into the lake of fire (Revelation 19).

Revelation 20:1–6 describes a period known as the millennial kingdom. During this thousand-year period, God's people will dwell with him while Satan and those with him will be bound. Satan will then launch one final attack, be defeated again, and be cast into the lake of fire at the end of Revelation 20.

Revelation 21–22, the final two chapters of the Bible, describe the new heavens, new earth, and New Jerusalem, where God will be with his people forever. There will be no more curse, sin, or death as believers dwell with the Lord for all eternity.

The two main areas of dispute among believers are the timing of the rapture and views of the millennial kingdom. We argue that there are too many differences in the passages about the rapture and second coming for them to all refer to the same event.

Regarding the millennial kingdom, some view the idea symbolically, arguing that it is an example of a day being like a thousand years (2 Peter 3:8). However, the thousand years being stated multiple times is important. In addition, this literal period allows the literal fulfillment of many prophecies of the Messiah reigning from David's throne in Jerusalem.

Many other details could be included and are discussed elsewhere in this book. However, this brief outline of rapture, tribulation, Christ's return, the millennial kingdom, and eternity future are the key aspects developed in Scripture that believers can focus on and look forward to as God fulfills his future promises.

29. What Are the Different Views of the Rapture?

Bible scholars often debate the sequence of end-time events, though they agree on the essential truth that Jesus will return to gather his people. The primary disagreement lies in the timing of this event, with the two main views being the pretribulation and posttribulation views of the rapture.

The pretribulation view argues that Jesus will return to rapture his followers before the onset of the seven-year tribulation. According to this view, the rapture is an event separate from the second coming of Christ at the end of the tribulation. In this scenario, Jesus will first take his people to heaven and later return with them to defeat his enemies and establish his millennial reign on earth.

In contrast, the posttribulation view holds that Jesus will only return once: at the end of the seven-year tribulation. Adherents of this view believe that Christians will endure the tribulation period, facing its trials and the reign of the Antichrist before Christ's final return to earth. This perspective argues that all Christians will experience the full duration of the tribulation before Jesus' return.

Both views have been supported by dedicated Bible scholars, many of whom provide compelling arguments. However, several reasons make the pretribulation view appear more plausible.

First, the differences between the passages describing the rapture and the second coming suggest they are distinct events. Key rapture passages, such as 1 Corinthians 15:51–58 and 1 Thessalonians 4:13–18, depict Jesus taking the dead in Christ and living believers to heaven. John 14 also describes Jesus taking his followers to the Father's house in heaven. In contrast, passages describing the second coming (such as those in Revelation) portray Jesus returning to earth with his followers to defeat his enemies. These differences indicate that the rapture and the second coming involve different events and purposes.

Second, the pretribulation view aligns well with the church's absence in Revelation 4–18. In this book, letters are sent to seven churches in chapters 1–3, but the church is notably absent from the tribulation scenes depicted in chapters 4–18. The church reappears only at the battle of Armageddon in chapter 19. This absence suggests that the church has already been taken to heaven, supporting the idea of a pretribulation rapture. During the tribulation, many Jews and some gentiles will come to faith in Christ, but the church will have already been raptured.

Third, the pretribulation view is consistent with the biblical teaching of Christ's imminent return. The concept of imminence, or the belief that Jesus could return at any moment, fits well with the idea of a pretribulation rapture. If Christians were to endure a seven-year tribulation before being taken to heaven, it would undermine the notion of Christ's imminent return. The pretribulation view underscores the importance of living a life of readiness and anticipation, as Jesus' return could happen at any moment.

Paul's encouragement in 1 Thessalonians 4:18 (to "comfort one another with these words") highlights the comfort and hope provided by the pretribulation view. In contrast, a posttribulation view, which involves enduring seven years of tribulation, might not offer the same level of comfort. Knowing that Jesus could return at any moment provides believers with a hopeful and exciting anticipation of being in the Lord's presence forever.

30. WILL PEOPLE BE SAVED AFTER THE RAPTURE?

Some teachers have claimed that no one will be able to believe in Jesus after the rapture. Is this true?

A close look at Scripture reveals that many people will believe in Christ after the rapture. After the rapture, a seven-year tribulation period will unfold before Jesus comes to defeat his enemies at the battle of Armageddon (Revelation 19). During this tribulation, one prediction noted is the conversion of many Jews to faith in Jesus as the Messiah.

In Revelation 7, a group of one hundred forty-four thousand Jews will lead in sharing the Messiah, indicating that hundreds of thousands of Jews will come to faith during this time.

In Revelation 6:9–10, we also find an account of people who will be killed for their faith during the tribulation: "When He opened the fifth seal, I saw under the altar the souls of those who had been slain for the word of God and for the testimony which they held. And they cried with a loud voice, saying, 'How long, O Lord, holy and true, until You judge and avenge our blood on those who dwell on the earth?'"

Both Jews and gentiles will come to faith in the Lord following the rapture, but their lives will not be easy. The catastrophes of the tribulation period will impact both believers and unbelievers living during that time, with large numbers of deaths and widespread disasters. In addition, persecution will be stronger during this time. In addition to the martyrs mentioned in Revelation 6, those who refuse to receive the mark of the beast will be unable to buy or sell anything (Revelation 13).

Revelation 11 describes the death of two witnesses who will speak for the Lord in Jerusalem. Their treatment may represent the treatment of other believers during this time. They were killed for their beliefs, with unbelievers rejoicing at their deaths. In their case, the Lord resurrects them, but the way they are persecuted points to the difficulties those who believe will face during the tribulation.

The popular *Left Behind* book series and related films seek to portray some of the challenges people will face when they believe after the rapture. There is still hope, but there will also be struggles far beyond what believers face today.

A look at the treatment of believers and the disasters of the tribulation shows that it is easier to believe in Jesus now than to wait until after the rapture. However, it is also important to note that God's grace even extends to many who will believe during this future time of conflict and suffering, offering salvation to all who believe.

31. WHAT IS THE PARTIAL RAPTURE VIEW AND IS IT BIBLICAL?

The rapture is the belief that Jesus is coming at any moment to take believers to be with him in heaven forever. However, there is also a little-known theory that some have questions about called the "partial rapture view." What is it, and is there any truth to this perspective?

The partial rapture view argues that only some believers will be taken to be with the Lord upon his return. The idea is largely based on Matthew 25:1–13 and the interpretation of the wise and foolish virgins. Those who argue for a partial rapture view believe that this passage teaches that only Christians who are prepared for Christ's return will be raptured while others will remain to face the sufferings of the tribulation period.

The one other verse usually cited by proponents of this view is 1 John 2:28: "Now, little children, abide in Him, that when He appears, we may have confidence and not be ashamed before Him at His coming." Those holding the partial rapture view claim that only those who are not ashamed will be taken to be with the Lord. Others will be left behind, suffering death during the tribulation or living through the rapture until Christ returns after the seven-year tribulation at the battle of Armageddon (Revelation 19).

This obscure view was popularized in a book by Robert Govett in 1853 and was later taught by a prophecy teacher named G. H. Lang in the twentieth century. It has not been widely held, and for good reasons.

The late prophecy expert Dr. John Walvoord explains that there are three reasons this view should be rejected.[6] First, the partial rapture view is grounded in a works-based approach that conflicts with scriptural teachings on grace. According to these teachings, the translation of the church (moving believers from earth to heaven as described in John 14:1–3) and the resurrection of the church are part of its salvation granted through grace, and these events are considered a reward only in the sense that they are the result of faith in Christ.

Adopting a works-based principle for this aspect of salvation undermines the concept of justification by faith through grace, the role of the Holy Spirit as God's seal "for the day of redemption" (Ephesians 4:30), and the immense effort by God on behalf of those who trust him. The issue of reward is rightly addressed at the judgment seat of Christ, not through a partial translation that results in tribulation affecting other believers.

Second, the partial rapture view causes a division within the body of Christ. While the Bible does indicate differences in God's dealings with Old Testament saints compared to those of

---

6 John F. Walvoord, "Premillennialism and the Tribulation—Part V: Partial Rapture Theory," Bible.org, January 1, 2008, https://bible.org.

the current age or between the church and tribulation saints, there is no biblical basis for separating the unified body of Christ

The third issue with the partial rapture view is that it disregards the clear biblical teaching that all true believers will be translated together at the event of the rapture (1 Corinthians 15:51–58; 1 Thessalonians 4:13–18). The rapture is a one-time event for all believers, not an experience for a group of spiritually elite saints.

32. What Is the Marriage Supper of the Lamb?

Revelation 19 mentions the marriage supper of the Lamb. Those who participate in it are blessed. What is this future event?

The marriage supper of the Lamb refers to the traditions of a Jewish wedding. The event included three major parts. The first aspect was the dowry. This was an agreement between the parents of the bride and groom that included a payment to the bride or her family.

The second part of Jewish marriage included the groom arriving at the bride's home late at night. The groom and his friends would arrive with torches as part of the ceremony for the bride. An example of this part of the Jewish marriage tradition is described in Matthew 25, where Jesus tells the parable of the ten virgins.

The third part was the actual marriage feast that traditionally lasted multiple days. For example, when Jesus turned water into wine during a wedding in Cana, the people had been feasting for a long time prior to the miracle (John 2:1–2).

In Revelation 19:6–8, John describes the future fulfillment of the wedding feast:

> I heard, as it were, the voice of a great multitude, as the sound of many waters and as the sound of mighty thunderings, saying, "Alleluia! For the Lord God Omnipotent reigns! Let us be glad and rejoice and give Him glory, for the marriage of the Lamb has come, and His wife has made herself ready." And to her it was granted to be arrayed in fine linen, clean and bright, for the fine linen is the righteous acts of the saints.

In this passage, the preparations had been made, and the time had come for the groom (Jesus) to arrive for his bride (his people). The bride has been made pure, and the celebration is ready to begin. Verse 9 adds, "Then he said to me, 'Write: "Blessed are those who are called to the marriage supper of the Lamb!"' And he said to me, 'These are the true sayings of God.'" Those who are called or are invited to this event will be blessed.

The discussion of the marriage supper of the Lamb is followed by Jesus coming on a white horse in victory to earth (v. 11). He defeats his enemies (chapters 17–21) and begins his millennial reign on his throne (20:1–6).

There is some dispute over whether the bride refers to believers taken to heaven during the rapture, people who believe during the tribulation, or both. Others argue for a posttribulation view of the rapture. In this view, Christ both returns for believers and defeats his enemies during the same set of events.

The phrase "His wife has made herself ready" appears to describe a time of preparation. Those who hold to a pretribulation view usually argue that the church is in heaven after the rapture and is "made ready" before Christ comes in Revelation 19. One's view of the rapture usually influences the decision on this view as well. The main focus is that the wedding supper of the Lamb is the fulfillment of Christ's return to live with his people in unity. It is a time for all believers to look forward to with great anticipation.

33. What Will Happen to Pets After the Rapture?

Several years ago, a business claimed to provide pet insurance services for Christians to care for their animals after the rapture. The service claimed to charge hundreds of people over $100 each. The elaborate account was later revealed as a hoax. The issue, however, did bring up an important question for many Christian pet lovers: What will happen to their pets after the rapture?

First, pets will not go to heaven in the rapture. The coming of Jesus is for believers, not for their animals. God created animals and cares for them, but his coming is for those humans created in his image who have believed in his name for salvation.

Second, pets will continue to live as normal on earth after the rapture and throughout the tribulation period. There is no biblical reason to believe animals will suddenly experience life differently, other than that they will have to face the same disasters the rest of the world will face during the tribulation period.

Third, some predictions during the tribulation note a terrible future for many animals. For example, Revelation 8:7 reveals a time when a third of the trees will be burned up. This will cause widespread problems and death for land animals and birds. In verse 8, the seas are struck, and a third of all sea creatures die. In verse 10, a third of all water will be polluted, harming many pets and other animals.

Despite the coming judgments on the earth during the rapture, many pets will simply fall into the care of those nearest them. Some will experience the loving care of a neighbor or friend while others will be left to care for themselves.

It is certainly concerning to consider leaving our dogs, cats, or other pets behind when Christ comes. However, we can take comfort in God's perfect wisdom and judgment. He created our pets and has blessed us with them during this time in our lives. The Lord also knows how to best handle the many pets left behind in Christian homes following the rapture.

Much about animals in the afterlife is left unaddressed in Scripture. However, the Bible does describe some animals in the future. Isaiah 11 describes wolves and lambs dwelling together in the future millennial kingdom, along with leopards, goats, cows, lions, oxen, and even vipers. When God creates a new heaven and new earth (Revelation 21–22), animals of many kinds will likely serve as part of our eternal future home.

SECTION 5

THE ANTICHRIST AND THE FALSE PROPHET

34. WHO IS THE ANTICHRIST?

The Antichrist is prophesied as a future global ruler who will control the kingdoms of the earth and persecute Christians during the tribulation period. The question of when this Antichrist will appear—and whether he might already be alive—intrigues many.

The most detailed descriptions of the Antichrist's role and actions are found in Daniel 7–12, 2 Thessalonians 2, and Revelation 13, with Revelation 13 providing the most comprehensive account.

Scripture offers various insights into the identity and nature of the Antichrist. Daniel 9:26 refers to him as "the prince who is to come," while 2 Thessalonians 2:3 describes him as a "man of lawlessness" and "son of destruction" (NIV). This individual will be marked by lawlessness, deceit, and destruction, and he will emerge as an intimidating global leader.

The term "Antichrist" appears four times in the New Testament (1 John 2:18, 22; 4:3; 2 John 1:7). This figure is characterized by a denial of Christ, and John notes that many antichrists were already present in his time (1 John 2:18). The spirit of antichrist is found in one who denies Jesus' incarnation, deity, and exclusivity as the one true Messiah. So someone who says that Jesus is a way to God but not *the* way has the mindset of antichrist. The same is true for someone who claims that Jesus was a good man but not God. Such antichrists are with us today, and they were around in the apostle John's time.

But there is one who will have this antichrist spirit who will be *the* Antichrist. He will be demonically empowered and the enemy of God. He will try to rule the world. This eventual full and final Antichrist will be a faux incarnation—not God in human form (as Jesus was) but Satan incarnate.

The Antichrist will eventually become a prominent leader from modern Europe who will negotiate a peace agreement with Israel and exhibit other specific traits outlined in Revelation 13.

According to Revelation 13, the Antichrist will be male and is described as coming from a revived Roman Empire. He will seek to unify religions while ultimately demanding worship for himself. His reign will be marked by deceit and authoritarianism, culminating in an imposition of the mark of the beast on his followers.

Key characteristics of the Antichrist include his apparent recovery from a fatal wound and his enforcement of the mark of the beast, represented by the number 666. Revelation 13 describes him as surviving a mortal wound and then gaining even greater power. Furthermore, he will compel all people to receive a mark on their right hand or forehead, without which they cannot buy or sell any goods.

The Antichrist will also be a man of war, waging persecution against believers during the tribulation. Revelation 13:7 highlights his authority over every tribe, tongue, and nation as he makes war with the saints and overcomes them. His regime will be marked by severe oppression, particularly against those who uphold faith in God, including Jews.

Second Thessalonians 2 describes the Antichrist as "the man of lawlessness…the son of destruction, who opposes and exalts himself against every so-called god or object of worship, so that he takes his seat in the temple of God, proclaiming himself to be God" (vv. 3–4 ESV).

The timing of the Antichrist's appearance is debated among Christians. Those who believe in a pretribulation rapture expect the Antichrist to emerge after Jesus' return to gather his followers. This Antichrist would then confirm a seven-year peace treaty with Israel. Conversely, those who believe the rapture will occur at the end of the tribulation might expect the Antichrist's activities to unfold concurrently with or lead up to Christ's return.

Regardless of one's end-time view on this issue, the Antichrist may be already alive today. However, there is no need for believers to fear this future figure. Instead, we should remain vigilant for all individuals who deny Christ. We should also focus on Christ and remain steadfast in our faith as we await Christ's promised return.

35. Who is the Beast of Revelation?

Revelation describes multiple beasts, leaving some confusion regarding their identity in Bible prophecy. Who is the beast of Revelation?

Revelation 13:1–2 describes the key beast who will arise during the future tribulation:

> Then I stood on the sand of the sea. And I saw a beast rising up out of the sea, having seven heads and ten horns, and on his horns ten crowns, and on his heads a blasphemous name. Now the beast which I saw was like a leopard, his feet were like *the feet of* a bear, and his mouth like the mouth of a lion. The dragon gave him his power, his throne, and great authority.

This first beast is a group of nations that will deceive people into following the Antichrist during the tribulation period. The beast appears to include either the leaders of a revived Roman Empire or will represent global leaders united with the Antichrist.

A second beast is also mentioned in Revelation and is also referred to as the false prophet. Revelation 13:11 says, "Then I saw another beast coming up out of the earth, and he had two horns like a lamb and spoke like a dragon."

This second beast will have great authority and will force people to worship the first beast (v. 12). He will also perform "great signs" (vv. 13–15). Another important aspect of the false prophet's work will be to enforce the mark of the beast used by people to buy or sell.

These beasts will be allowed to rule during the tribulation period, but their time in power will be short. At the end of the seven-year tribulation, Jesus will defeat his enemies and cast the beasts into the lake of fire. The beasts will join one final rebellion at the end of Christ's one-thousand-year millennial kingdom and be defeated again. They will then be cast into the lake of fire with Satan forever (20:7–10).

Some have also described the false prophet as part of an "unholy trinity" consisting of Satan, the Antichrist, and the false prophet. These three leaders will serve in key roles in the end times to deceive people despite clear evidence of God's judgment upon the earth. This unholy trinity will represent the opposite of the Holy Trinity consisting of the Father, Son, and Holy Spirit. These evil beings will turn people away from God yet will ultimately fail in their quest for power.

In the new heavens and new earth, all evil and the curse of sin will be removed. God will dwell with his people for all eternity while the false prophet and those who have rebelled with him will experience eternal punishment.

36. WHAT IS THE MARK OF THE BEAST?

The enigmatic "mark of the beast" is outlined in Revelation 13:16–18:

> He causes all, both small and great, rich and poor, free and slave, to receive a mark on their right hand or on their foreheads, and that no one may buy or sell except one who has the mark or the name of the beast, or the number of his name. Here is wisdom. Let him who has understanding calculate the number of the beast, for it is the number of a man: His number is 666.

Understanding this mark involves delving into several factors regarding its significance.

First, the mark will be a visible identifier on either the forehead or the right hand, which will be crucial for engaging in economic transactions. Although this prophecy points to a future event, some view contemporary technological advancements as potential precursors. For instance, the move toward a cashless society could foreseeably lead to transactions facilitated through wearable devices, such as wristbands, tattoos, or even implants. In addition, technologies like optical scans or even smart glasses might align with the concept of a mark on the forehead.

Second, the number 666 is described as "the number of a man," which suggests a connection to a specific individual—a future global leader known as the Antichrist. In ancient times, currency often bore the image of the ruling emperor, so similarly, future monetary systems might bear the mark of this Antichrist. This mark would serve as a symbol of allegiance to this powerful figure, who will rise to prominence during the prophesied seven-year tribulation.

Furthermore, the mark of the beast is part of a broader end-times deception. Revelation 13:14 indicates that the beast performs signs that deceive the earth's inhabitants. Those who accept the mark will be misled by the Antichrist, believing in his false promises and authority.

The mark will also serve as a testament to one's allegiance to the Antichrist. As this global leader will control all commerce, accepting the mark—often under the mistaken belief that he will establish world peace—will signify support for him. Those deceived into taking the mark will demonstrate their loyalty to the Antichrist.

On the other hand, those who refuse to accept the mark will face persecution. This will likely include Jews, who, due to their faith in one God, will reject the mark. Similarly, Christians who come to faith during the tribulation will resist the mark, recognizing the Antichrist as a malevolent force.

Some interpretations link the number 666 to historical figures such as Nero, suggesting a connection to the Antichrist and a revived Roman Empire as described in Scripture. However, these connections remain speculative.

Despite these interpretations and potential future implications, believers today need not fear accidentally taking the mark of the beast. The current era is not the time of the tribulation when the mark will be enforced.

Instead, Christians are encouraged to remain vigilant and steadfast in their faith, trusting in the promise of Jesus' return before the onset of these prophesied events. Contemporary technologies may hint at future possibilities, but they should not incite fear in believers who are assured of their salvation and Christ's coming at the rapture.

37. WHAT IS THE MEANING OF THE NUMBER 666 IN THE BIBLE?

Revelation 13:18 describes the mark of the beast, stating, "Here is wisdom. Let him who has understanding calculate the number of the beast, for it is the number of a man: His number is 666." What is the meaning of this number?

The significance of the number 666 has fascinated people for centuries and is frequently linked with Satan. While popular culture often associates it with horror, some individuals avoid the number out of fear. Gematria, a method that assigns numerical values to Hebrew letters, has also been used in attempts to decipher the meaning behind 666. This practice has linked the number to Nero or modern world leaders.

Biblically, 666 is less about encoding the Antichrist's name and more about symbolizing his character. During the end times, people will be required to receive the mark of the beast on their foreheads or hands to engage in commerce. Those who refuse will face persecution by the Antichrist while those who accept the mark will incur God's judgment. The mark represents allegiance to the Antichrist over God, and it is tied to the name or number of the beast.

Throughout the Bible, numbers carry symbolic meaning. Seven, for instance, signifies completeness and perfection and appears over seven hundred times, including as the number of days in creation.

Similarly, 666 is symbolic; John refers to it as the "number of man," representing imperfection. Created on the sixth day and having sinned against God, humanity is incomplete without divine guidance. The Antichrist will attempt to replace God, seeking to elevate himself and demand worship. However, the combined forces of the Antichrist, false prophet, and Satan will ultimately be defeated by Jesus (Revelation 19–20).

Another interesting parallel is found in 1 Kings 10:14. The weight of the gold that came to King Solomon each year was 666 talents. Revelation may be using this number to reflect an emphasis on a leader's money or greed, though this is uncertain.

Christians should not be fearful or overly concerned with 666. Jesus has already triumphed over sin, and with his Spirit dwelling within us, we have overcome the general spirit of the Antichrist and can trust in Jesus' supremacy over worldly forces (1 John 4:4). Ultimately, 666 exposes the Antichrist for what he is—a deceiver and impostor.

38. CAN A PERSON TAKE THE MARK OF THE BEAST AFTER BECOMING A CHRISTIAN OR BECOME A CHRISTIAN AFTER TAKING THE MARK?

One debate about the end times is the relationship between the mark of the beast and believing in Jesus. Can a person take the mark of the beast after becoming a believer, or can a person become a believer after taking the mark?

Revelation 14:9–12 addresses this issue:

> Then a third angel followed them, saying with a loud voice, "If anyone worships the beast and his image, and receives his mark on his forehead or on his hand, he himself shall also drink of the wine of the wrath of God, which is poured out full strength into the cup of His indignation. He shall be tormented with fire and brimstone in the presence of the holy angels and in the presence of the Lamb. And the smoke of their torment ascends forever and ever; and they have no rest day or night, who worship the beast and his image, and whoever receives the mark of his name." Here is the patience of the saints; here are

> those who keep the commandments of God and the faith of Jesus.

These words appear to clearly indicate that anyone who takes the mark will not later become a believer. A person will not accidentally take the mark but will do so as an act of allegiance to the Antichrist.

Revelation 16:2 also adds that judgment will target those with the mark. This judgment adds further evidence that only unbelievers will have this mark. Revelation 19:20–21 further notes the judgment upon those with the mark:

> Then the beast was captured, and with him the false prophet who worked signs in his presence, by which he deceived those who received the mark of the beast and those who worshiped his image. These two were cast alive into the lake of fire burning with brimstone. And the rest were killed with the sword which proceeded from the mouth of Him who sat on the horse. And all the birds were filled with their flesh.

Those who take the mark will be killed and cast into the lake of fire, meaning they are all unbelievers. In contrast, no true believer will take the mark of the beast during the tribulation.

It is important to remember that Christians today cannot take the mark of the beast. The rapture will happen first, with those taking the mark of the beast doing so starting at the midpoint of the seven-year tribulation. We do not need to worry about accidentally taking it or fear that the mark of the beast could be some form of technology or vaccine.

Instead, we are to focus on serving the Lord and helping others believe in him. Those left behind during the tribulation will face great suffering, with many deceived into taking the mark and eventually condemned to eternal judgment.

39. CAN A PERSON ACCIDENTALLY TAKE THE MARK OF THE BEAST?

As we discussed in the last question, the mark of the beast will occur during the tribulation period following the rapture. Those who believe will refuse to take the mark, while unbelievers who take the mark and worship the beast will experience judgment. But can a person accidentally take the mark of the beast?

First, the timeline of the mark of the beast removes any concerns that someone could take the mark of the beast today. The enforcement of the mark will not come until after the rapture and will become a major focus only in the second half of the seven-year tribulation.

Second, the nature of the mark will be obvious. It will be a mark on the right hand or forehead. “He causes all, both small and great, rich and poor, free and slave, to receive a mark on their right hand or on their foreheads,” Revelation 13:16 states.

In some ways, this evil mark is a contrast with God’s commands to remember his words found in Deuteronomy 6:8: “You shall bind them as a sign on your hand, and they shall be as frontlets between your eyes.” Just as the Israelites were to literally carry God’s words on their wrist and forehead, the mark of the beast will be a clear external mark that no one will take by accident.

Third, the mark will be taken by those who worship the beast. Those who refuse to worship the beast will face death: “He was granted power to give breath to the image of the beast, that the image of the beast should both speak and cause as many as would not worship the image of the beast to be killed" (Revelation 13:15). The consequences will be clear and severe. There will be no mistakes over who takes the mark.

While the mark of the beast will be taken intentionally, it is reasonable to have concerns about the invasive nature of some of today's technologies. For example, our smartphones, watches, and many cars track our travel, heart rate, spending, search history, and much more.

Our growing digital culture is also leading to a more cashless society in which finances are controlled electronically. Those with the right tools or access have great power, as they are able to manipulate everything from a person's checking account to global markets.

A healthy skepticism of external tracking and controls can be wise, but there is no need to fear that we will somehow accidentally take the mark of the beast. This future choice will be clear to those who take it, involving an unprecedented deception that will lead many astray.

40. What Is the Image of the Beast?

Two beasts are mentioned in Revelation 13. The first represents a group of nations under the influence of the Antichrist. The second beast is the false prophet. But what is the image of the beast?

The false prophet will make this image that is described in verses 14–15:

> He deceives those who dwell on the earth by those signs which he was granted to do in the sight of the beast, telling those who dwell on the earth to make

> an image to the beast who was wounded by the sword and lived. He was granted power to give breath to the image of the beast, that the image of the beast should both speak and cause as many as would not worship the image of the beast to be killed.

This lifelike image will be some type of manipulated force that is made to look real. In ancient Babylon, Shadrach, Meshech, and Abednego faced death after refusing to bow down to a massive image created by King Nebuchadnezzar. They were thrown into the fiery furnace and supernaturally rescued by the Lord (Daniel 3). Until recent times, most Bible teachers believed the false prophet's image of the beast would be something similar.

With today's technologies, many other options exist. For example, some of Japan's top pop stars have been holograms in recent years. Hatsune Miku was released in 2007 as a Vocaloid (a product of voice synthesizing software) whose voice and image are all computer-generated. In addition, hologram technologies now allow a high level of realism to make images look alive, with some media experts predicting hologram tours as the future of live concerts.

Other suggestions for what the image of the beast will be included a robotic image due to the realistic versions of robots now in development. Still others have mentioned the possibility of a human clone, though this is unlikely since the focus is on an "image" rather than an actual copy of human life.

The apostle John wrote based on the vision he received. We have a record of the words God inspired him to write based on what John could explain in the language of his time. It may not address all modern details about this future image, but the outcome was the most concerning focus.

One major distinction is that those who reject worshiping the future image of the beast will be killed. It is uncertain whether the image is involved in killing those who reject worshiping it or if, more likely, such rejection leads to the sentence of death.

If the parallel to Daniel 3 is similar, most will bow down in worship while a small number will refuse to worship the image and will be sentenced to death. Those who choose the Lord over the image will be obedient to the commandment to not bow down to idols (Exodus 20:4–5) but will face martyrdom for their decision.

It may be difficult to determine the exact nature of this image today, but the concern is one for those on the earth during the tribulation, a time believers will avoid because they will be with the Lord at the rapture (1 Thessalonians 4:13–18).

41. What Is the Abomination of Desolation?

Jesus mentions the abomination of desolation in his message about the future in Matthew 24:15. What is this event? Has it already occurred or is this a prediction about the future?

"'Therefore when you see the "abomination of desolation," spoken of by Daniel the prophet, standing in the holy place' (whoever reads, let him understand), 'then let those who are in Judea flee to the mountains,'" Matthew recorded in verses 15–16. Verses 21–22 add, "'For then there will be great tribulation, such as has not been since the beginning of the world until this time, no, nor ever shall be. And unless those days were shortened, no flesh would be saved; but for the elect's sake those days will be shortened.'"

The words appear to refer to a yet-future event. Jesus referred to the same prediction noted by Daniel in 11:31 and 12:11. In Daniel 11, this abomination occurs at the midpoint of the tribulation. Daniel 12:11 says there will be 1,290 days after this abomination, a reference to the second half of the tribulation period.

While the timing of the event clearly appears to occur at the midpoint of the tribulation, it is more difficult to understand what this abomination is. Daniel 11:31 says, "Forces shall be mustered by him, and they shall defile the sanctuary fortress; then they shall take away the daily sacrifices, and place there the abomination of desolation." These words describe a leader (the Antichrist) ending the Jewish ritual temple sacrifices and replacing them with something else.

Daniel 9:27 adds that this will be a time when the sacrifices and offerings end. At the midpoint of the tribulation, Revelation 13:14–15 says:

> He deceives those who dwell on the earth by those signs which he was granted to do in the sight of the beast, telling those who dwell on the earth to make an image to the beast who was wounded by the sword and lived. He was granted power to give breath to the image of the beast, that the image of the beast should both speak and cause as many as would not worship the image of the beast to be killed.

The abomination of desolation may include both ending temple sacrifices and forcing people to worship the image of the beast.

In Jewish history, Antiochus IV (Epiphanes), the king of Syria, sacrificed a pig in the Jewish temple to desecrate it. He also set up an idol of Zeus in the Jewish temple. These actions appear to foreshadow the types of actions that will occur in the future abomination of desolation. The temple will be rebuilt before the midpoint of the tribulation, with the Antichrist defiling it and ending ritual sacrifice. He will require all people to bow down to the image, demanding that all people take the mark of the beast to buy or sell the things they need.

These events reflect past rejections of God and foretell even greater judgments upon the earth during the difficult time of the tribulation when the Antichrist will rule with a strong hand against the people of the earth. His power will be limited, however, as Christ will return at the end of the tribulation to defeat those who oppose him and set up his millennial kingdom with all of his followers.

42. Will the Antichrist Be Gay or LGBTQ?

Due to a description in the book of Daniel, some people have asked us if the future Antichrist will be gay or part of the LGBTQ community. Is this possible?

Daniel 11:37, the key verse on the topic, reads, "He shall regard neither the God of his fathers nor the desire of women, nor regard any god; for he shall exalt himself above them all."

What does the phrase "nor the desire of women" mean? Does this mean the Antichrist will not desire relationships with women?

Other translations render this phrase differently. For example, the English Standard Version (ESV) reads "or to the one beloved by women." Similar wording is also found in the NIV. Still other translations render the words "the god loved by women,"[7] emphasizing that the Antichrist will show no regard for any other god.

Even Hebrew scholars differ in determining the best translation of this phrase into English. While it is possible that the Antichrist will be either LGBTQ or asexual, the interpretation is not definitive. The focus instead may be on the Antichrist rejecting all other gods in favor of declaring himself as a god.

The LGBTQ emphasis in modern culture opposes the teachings of God's Word for human sexuality. God created male and female to live within the covenant of marriage between one man and one woman, according to the example found in Genesis 1–2. In Matthew 19:1–10, Jesus answered a question regarding divorce by affirming marriage between one man and one woman as God's design.

In the Old Testament, the Mosaic law included harsh punishments for sexual sins, including same-sex activity. In the New Testament, Paul opposed same-sex activity (Romans 1:26–27), calling it wrong (1 Corinthians 6:9–10). Jude 1:7 calls it immoral.

Interestingly, in Paul's list of sinful actions that included same-sex activity in 1 Corinthians 6:7–11, he concluded with the words, "Such were some of you. But you were washed, but

---

7 See, for example, the New English Translation (NET) and the New Living Translation (NLT).

you were sanctified, but you were justified in the name of the Lord Jesus and by the Spirit of our God." A person involved in same-sex activity is called to turn to the Lord and live differently by the Spirit of God.

The church has been known for sometimes mistreating people who identify as LGBTQ, acting like such lifestyles are a special "worse" category of sin. Instead, Scripture calls believers to share the gospel with those in such situations and help them live for the Lord in purity and righteousness.

The Antichrist will certainly oppose God's plan for human sexuality, but it is unclear whether he will personally participate in any kind of LGBTQ relationship. The emphasis is instead on his opposition to God, which will lead to his doom when Christ returns.

43. What Will the Antichrist's Religion Be?

Many people have wondered what the Antichrist's religion will be. Could he be a Muslim, a Buddhist, some other religion, or even an atheist?

Daniel 11:36–39 describes some of the future actions regarding the Antichrist that deal with his religion:

> "Then the king shall do according to his own will: he shall exalt and magnify himself above every god, shall speak blasphemies against the God of gods, and shall prosper till the wrath has been accomplished; for what has been determined shall be done. He shall regard neither the God of his fathers nor the desire of

> women, nor regard any god; for he shall exalt himself above them all" (vv. 36–37).

Taken literally, this future Antichrist will declare himself as god and oppose the God of the Bible. This would include rejecting Judaism and Christianity along with any form of monotheism, such as Islam. Instead, the focus of the Antichrist will be on the material world. Verse 38 notes, "But in their place he shall honor a god of fortresses."

This verse also mentions that "a god which his fathers did not know he shall honor with gold and silver, with precious stones and pleasant things." Verse 39 adds, "He shall act against the strongest fortresses with a foreign god, which he shall acknowledge, and advance its glory; and he shall cause them to rule over many, and divide the land for gain."

Two competing ideas are in operation in this passage. First, the Antichrist views himself as a god. However, he will also honor a god of fortresses. It is highly unlikely that this god of fortresses refers to Islam or another major world religion. Instead, the emphasis is likely secular, emphasizing human accomplishment and denying the power of the one true God.

The idea of a Muslim Antichrist has been popularized by a few writers in recent years. However, the arguments are not convincing. The biblical background of the Antichrist points to a leader of a revived Roman Empire. The Antichrist will also be male, according to the pronouns used to describe him.

The closest thing in the Bible that even potentially points to a Muslim Antichrist would be a global leader from a Muslim background in Europe (the revived Roman Empire) who rejects his former religion. In this sense, it could only be a person of Muslim background, not someone who practices traditional Islam.

Islam does have its own teachings regarding the end times, including a large branch of Islam popular in Iran known as Shia Islam, whose teachings predict that the Twelfth Imam, or twelfth descendant of Muhammad, will return in the last days. However, this is far different than a Muslim Antichrist, a view that lacks biblical support.

44. WHY DO SOME PEOPLE CLAIM THE POPE WILL BE THE ANTICHRIST?

Over the centuries, some people have suggested that the pope of the Roman Catholic Church is the future Antichrist. Why do some people believe the pope will be the leader of the world in the last days?

To be clear, we do not believe Scripture teaches this view. However, it is easy to understand why some people have held this perspective. The idea largely comes from Revelation 17:9 which says, "Here is the mind which has wisdom: The seven heads are seven mountains on which the woman sits." Since Rome is built on seven hills, it is identified as the location of the Antichrist, with the pope as the leader of this location.

Others view the leader of the Roman Catholic Church as the future world ruler of all religions. This is based on the size and influence of the Catholic Church and the prediction of a one-world government led by an Antichrist. However, the Antichrist is predicted to be a global leader who will desecrate the Jewish temple and set himself up as a god.

The future Antichrist will also be known in this way: "By this you know the Spirit of God: Every spirit that confesses that Jesus Christ has come in the flesh is of God, and every spirit that does not confess that Jesus Christ has come in the flesh is not of God. And this is the spirit of the Antichrist, which you have heard was coming, and is now already in the world" (1 John 4:2–3). The Antichrist will clearly oppose a literal Messiah.

The teachings of the Roman Catholic Church and every pope have confessed Jesus as the Christ. While there are differences between Catholic and Protestant teachings, it is difficult to claim the Antichrist will be the same person who holds to the creed of Jesus as God's one and only Son.

It is important, however, to note the influence of Rome and of religion in general in the future. The final kingdom predicted by Daniel will be a revived Roman Empire. The future religion of the tribulation period will be led by the Antichrist. He will reject God and traditional religion, setting himself up as god.

The Antichrist will also have a future false prophet (Revelation 13:11–17). It is more likely that this prophet will be associated with a traditional religion and perhaps even be a leader like the pope. If so, it would require a leader who rejects Jesus as God's Son.

While there are some connections between Rome and the future Antichrist, the pope is a highly unlikely candidate. Instead, a strong political leader will arise as the one who will deceive the nations in the last days ahead of God's coming judgment.

45. WHO IS THE MAN OF LAWLESSNESS?

In discussing the end times, 2 Thessalonians 2:3–4 warns, "Let no one deceive you by any means; for that Day will not come unless the falling away comes first, and the man of sin [or man of lawlessness] is revealed, the son of perdition, who opposes and exalts himself above all that is called God or that is worshiped, so that he sits as God in the temple of God, showing himself that he is God." Who is this man of lawlessness?

The "man of lawlessness" (v. 3 NIV) refers to the Antichrist, who is expected to emerge on the global stage after the rapture of the church (1 Thessalonians 4:13–18). The term "that Day" denotes the "day of the Lord" (Zechariah 14:1), which encompasses seven years of tribulation, Jesus' return to confront and defeat the rebellion, his one-thousand-year reign on earth, the final defeat of Satan, and the great white throne judgment.

This figure, described in Daniel 7 as a king who will try to overturn all that honors God, will defy God's law. With his charismatic presence and what many will perceive as miracles, he will attract people with promises of global peace through political, financial, and religious unity. Israel will enter into a seven-year covenant with him, but this covenant will ultimately last only three-and-a-half years (Daniel 9:27).

The man of lawlessness will proclaim himself as God, enter the Jewish temple in Jerusalem, and demand to be worshiped (2 Thessalonians 2:4). Jesus referred to this period in Mark 13:14, stating, "'When you see the "abomination of desolation," spoken of by Daniel the prophet, standing where it ought not' (let the reader understand), 'then let those who are in Judea flee to the mountains.'"

Although this man of lawlessness is not Satan himself, he will act under Satan's influence. At the end of the tribulation, he will lead armies against Christ, the King of kings, in the battle of Armageddon (Revelation 19:19). When he and his false prophet are defeated, they will be thrown into the lake of fire (v. 20), while Jesus will live victoriously with his people forever (20:1–4).

In Scripture, only one other person besides the Antichrist is designated as the "son of destruction," and that is Judas Iscariot (John 17:12 ESV). This title is reserved for the two most notorious figures in history, both under Satan's influence (John 13:2; Revelation 13:2) and responsible for some of the gravest acts of betrayal. Judas had the unique experience of living and ministering alongside the incarnate Son of God for over three years—a privilege shared by only eleven others. Despite witnessing Jesus' perfect life, hearing his profound teachings, and experiencing his divine power and kindness, Judas chose to betray him.

The rise of lawlessness today should not surprise Christians, as 2 Timothy 3:13 predicts that "evil men and impostors will grow worse and worse, deceiving and being deceived." Many will be misled by the false hope offered by the man of lawlessness, and this misleading will end in their destruction.

SECTION 6

THE TRIBULATION

46. WHAT ARE THE DIFFERENT VIEWS OF THE TRIBULATION?

The Bible's prophecies speak of a time of future tribulation lasting seven years before the return of Jesus at his second coming. What are the different views of this future period?

Four main views have been developed over the years, though only two have dominated most discussions. The first view is the pretribulation view. This view, which we (the authors) hold, understands that Jesus will come to rapture believers to heaven before the seven-year tribulation. The main distinction includes viewing the rapture and second coming as two distinct events due to the many differences between them as described in Scripture.

The second common view is the posttribulation view. Defenders of this view believe that Jesus will come back at the end of the seven-year tribulation, rapture believers, and defeat his enemies in the same series of events. This view sees believers remaining on earth through the judgments of the tribulation period.

A third view that is less commonly held is the midtribulation view. This perspective holds that Jesus will rapture believers to heaven at the midpoint or three-and-a-half-year mark of the tribulation. A core idea in midtribulationism is that the "last trumpet" mentioned in 1 Corinthians 15:52 is the same as the trumpet described in Revelation 11:15. Since the trumpet in Revelation 11 is the final one in a series, this view identifies it as the "last trumpet" of 1 Corinthians 15.

This reasoning, though, overlooks the differing purposes of the trumpets. The trumpet associated with the rapture is referred to as "the trumpet call of God" (1 Thessalonians 4:16), signaling grace for the elect. The trumpet in Revelation 11 brings judgment. The seventh trumpet in Revelation is not the final trumpet in a chronological sense, as Matthew 24:31 refers to a trumpet that will sound later, signaling the start of Christ's reign.

The fourth view is the pre-wrath rapture view that teaches the rapture will occur before the opening of the seventh seal judgment late in the tribulation period. The pre-wrath rapture perspective interprets the trumpet and bowl judgments (Revelation 7–16) as manifestations of God's wrath, from which the church will be spared (1 Thessalonians 5:9). In contrast, the first six seal judgments (Revelation 6) are not seen as God's wrath but rather as the wrath of Satan or of the Antichrist. This interpretation is based on the fact that God's wrath is not explicitly mentioned until after the sixth seal is opened (Revelation 6:17).

All Bible-believing Christians believe Jesus is coming back, but many debate the timing of specific events. We argue that the best evidence supports Jesus coming at any moment for believers, sparing us from the wrath of the tribulation. This view also best accounts for the many differences between the Bible's descriptions of the rapture and second coming, offering a literal interpretation of end-time events that appears most consistent with the biblical evidence.

47. WHAT IS THE REVIVED ROMAN EMPIRE?

The revived Roman Empire is often used to describe a future global government that will emerge during the end times to rule much of the world. Although the term does not appear in the Bible, the Scriptures describe a powerful global government in Daniel and Revelation. This new empire is linked to the fourth beast described in Daniel 7. This beast, characterized by its ten horns and described as "dreadful and terrible, exceedingly strong" (Daniel 7:7), is generally seen as representing the Roman Empire (vv. 19–24).

A "little horn" emerging from among the ten horns (v. 8) is often associated with the Antichrist, suggesting a connection between this figure and the Roman Empire. Since this empire ended long ago, it is predicted that this empire will be revived during or by the time of the tribulation period.

The idea of the revived Roman Empire is also linked to the fifth kingdom in Daniel 2. This chapter recounts Nebuchadnezzar's dream of a statue made of various materials, with iron legs representing the Roman Empire and the feet, a mix of iron and clay, symbolizing the final world empire. The partial use of iron in the feet may imply that this last empire has connections to the Roman Empire. The ten toes of the statue may be the same as the ten horns in Daniel 7:20, potentially indicating a ten-nation alliance led by a ruler from Rome.

In Revelation 13, a ten-horned beast rising from the sea connects to the fourth beast in Daniel 7. This beast is depicted as blasphemous and oppressive, wielding global authority granted by Satan. This portrayal is often interpreted as a reference to a future political power or leader rather than a historical figure.

Some believe there is a connection between the European Union and the ten toes in Daniel 2 or the ten-horned beast in Daniel 7. The EU was formed in 1993, and some biblical scholars propose that it might be a precursor to the final world empire described in prophecy. However, this interpretation faces challenges, as the prophetic vision of a revived Roman Empire suggests a federation of ten kingdoms. As of this writing, the EU has nearly thirty member states.

Others have suggested a global group like the United Nations could better fit this future government and will be led by someone in the revived Roman Empire, perhaps even someone in Rome. While these suggestions are possible, it is unlikely that we will be able to determine which modern group of nations will fit these predictions until the tribulation.

We can discern signs of the time, but the details of these prophetic events remain unclear. It is important to understand what is coming, using this knowledge to focus on living for Christ and sharing him with those around us.

48. WHO IS MYSTERY BABYLON OR THE WHORE OF BABYLON?

Revelation 17:1 introduces the "great prostitute" sitting on many waters, while verse 5 identifies her with the title: "Mystery, Babylon the great, the mother of harlots, and of the abominations of the earth." Who is this figure often referred to as "Mystery, Babylon"?

The text describes this woman riding the scarlet beast, which represents the Antichrist, indicating that she is active during the seven-year tribulation period (v. 3). Verses 9–10 elaborate that the woman is associated with seven heads representing seven mountains and seven kings—five of whom have fallen, one of whom currently reigns, and one who is yet to come but will last only a short time.

The reference to "seven mountains" is commonly interpreted as Rome, known as the city of seven hills. This suggests that the woman is linked to Rome during the tribulation, potentially as part of a significant international coalition. Revelation 17:18 further clarifies that the woman represents a powerful city with dominion over the rulers of the earth. This reinforces the idea that she is a major city, likely Rome, which will embody this Babylon in the end times.

Additional support for this interpretation includes the expectation that the Antichrist will emerge from a revived Roman Empire and the fact that Rome has been referred to as Babylon since New Testament times (1 Peter 5:13). Some interpretations suggest the woman represents the Roman Catholic Church, but this view is more specific than Scripture supports, given the text primarily associates the woman with Rome and its role in leading the nations.

Ultimately, the woman is depicted as a city—a city closely connected with Rome. The city symbolizes an evil world system controlled by the Antichrist during the last days before Christ's return. The concept of "Mystery, Babylon" likely encompasses both political and religious dimensions, indicating a corrupt end-times regime marked by spiritual wickedness and ungodly practices.

Babylon is referenced 260 times in the Bible, making it the second most significant city after Jerusalem. Biblically, Babylon is often depicted as the city of the devil, in stark contrast to Jerusalem, which is regarded as God's city. The two cities are consistently portrayed in opposition.

Babylon represents a rebellion against God's salvation plan and symbolizes the first major international political and religious movement that has persisted in various forms throughout history. In contrast, Jerusalem embodies God's divine call to establish a nation and uphold his salvation plan and national identity for the world.

49. What Is the Global Religion of the End Times?

The Bible predicts a global system or religion that will arise in the last days. Revelation 17 describes a "great prostitute" or "great harlot," which is commonly interpreted as a symbol of a false religion that will emerge during the tribulation period. There has been considerable debate about which specific religion this might be, with some suggesting possibilities like the Roman Catholic Church, Islam, or another religious movement.

It is more likely that this false religion will be an inclusive, pluralistic system that embraces a broad view of God, potentially incorporating liberal monotheistic groups that see all religions as interconnected and are prepared to worship the Antichrist. This religion will likely reject any faith that is exclusive and opposed to the worship of the Antichrist or his image.

Revelation 17:6 depicts this false religion as being "drunk with the blood of the saints and with the blood of the martyrs of Jesus," indicating that it will not only tolerate but encourage the persecution and death of Christians during the tribulation. Verse 2 suggests that this false religion will be marked by sexual immorality and is expected to have its base in Rome, which was also referred to as Babylon in the New Testament (Revelation 17:5; 1 Peter 5:13).

Some believe this false religion will be short-lived since the Antichrist will demand worship of himself at the midpoint of the seven-year tribulation (Revelation 13). This religion may persist and incorporate worship of the Antichrist while opposing Christians and Jews, particularly as the Antichrist desecrates the temple (Matthew 24:15).

The deception during this period will be so profound that Jesus warned, "For false christs and false prophets will rise and show great signs and wonders to deceive, if possible, even the elect" (Matthew 24:24). There are also questions about whether such a one-world religion already exists in some form today. While the specific end-times religion cannot fully emerge until the Antichrist's rule during the tribulation, current trends toward religious pluralism, interfaith dialogue that equates all religions, and the idea that multiple paths lead to God or heaven do reflect early signs of this future scenario.

Revelation 17 depicts a religious system that reaches its peak during the first half of the tribulation but will be destroyed by a coalition of ten nations midway through the period. While the true church will have been raptured, apostate and false religions will persist and consolidate under a global system likely led by Rome.

As indicated by some of Jesus' parables in Matthew 13 and explicitly warned by Paul and Peter, the church age will see increasing apostasy (1 Timothy 4:1–3; 2 Timothy 3:13). This apostasy will manifest in the form of ecumenism, a movement aiming to merge all religions into a single system, potentially under Roman influence. To achieve this, the apostate religious system will use various strategies to establish a worldwide movement that will wield great influence in the last days.

50. Will There Be a One-World Government in the Last Days?

The increasing rise of globalism has led to many questions about its connections with Bible prophecy. Will there be a one-world government during the last days?

The Bible does not specifically mention a "one-world government," but it does present related concepts. For instance, the future Antichrist, referred to as "the beast" in Revelation, will wield significant global influence.

Revelation 13:3–4 describes how the entire world will be amazed and follow the beast, with people worshiping it and acknowledging its supreme power: "And I saw one of his heads as if it had been mortally wounded, and his deadly wound was healed. And all the world marveled and followed the beast. So they worshiped the dragon who gave authority to the beast; and they worshiped the beast, saying, 'Who is like the beast? Who is able to make war with him?'"

Verses 7–8 further note that the beast will have authority over every tribe, people, language, and nation, with everyone on earth worshiping it except for those whose names are written in the Book of Life: "It was granted to him to make war with the saints and to overcome them. And authority was given him over every tribe, tongue, and nation. All who dwell on the earth will worship him, whose names have not been written in the Book of Life of the Lamb slain from the foundation of the world."

While this suggests the Antichrist will have global dominance, it does not explicitly confirm the existence of a unified world government. The tribulation period is depicted as a time of great turmoil and conflict, and the precise nature of the governmental leadership is not given in full detail in Scripture.

There will also be a revived Roman Empire during the last days, according to predictions by Daniel. This final kingdom appears to control at least the area of the former Roman Empire and will serve as the hub of the future Antichrist. This kingdom will have global control, but it also appears that some will not submit to this leader and his kingdom.

During the tribulation, all who do not believe in Jesus will pledge their allegiance to the Antichrist. The requirement for buying or selling will be the mark of the beast (v. 17). Those who refuse the mark will face significant hardships, including persecution and scarcity, and could be punished by death.

Although the text implies global control, it does not necessarily confirm the presence of a formal one-world government.

The tribulation period will present severe challenges for those living during that time. Those who refuse to worship the Antichrist and reject his mark will endure great suffering. Despite these trials, those who turn to Christ during this period will maintain their faith and persevere. The Scriptures urge people to believe in Jesus now (John 3:16; Ephesians 2:8–9) to avoid the dire future described and to find salvation and eternal life with the Lord in heaven.

51. What Are the Ten Horns of the Beast in Revelation?

Revelation 13 provides a frightening look at the beast of Revelation, describing him as having ten horns and seven heads. What or who are these ten horns? What do they represent?

The beast represents the Antichrist, who will wield political power during the latter half of the great tribulation. This clarifies the significance of the ten horns. According to Daniel, "The ten horns are ten kings who shall arise from this kingdom" (Daniel 7:24).

Revelation aligns with this description, stating, "The ten horns which you saw are ten kings who have received no kingdom as yet, but they receive authority for one hour as kings with the beast. These are of one mind, and they will give their power and authority to the beast" (Revelation 17:12–13).

It is believed that the Antichrist will arise from a revived Roman Empire in the end times. This empire will be divided into ten regions, each ruled by a king who will govern under the Antichrist's authority. These ten kings, represented by the ten horns, will willingly yield their power to the Antichrist.

They will unite against Jesus (the Lamb) and his followers. Despite their considerable power, these ten kings will ultimately be defeated when Jesus returns:

> I saw the beast, the kings of the earth, and their armies, gathered together to make war against Him who sat on the horse and against His army. Then the beast was captured, and with him the false prophet who worked signs in his presence, by which he deceived those who received the mark of the beast and those who worshiped his image. These two were cast alive into the lake of fire burning with brimstone. (Revelation 19:19–20)

Many attempts have been made to identify these ten horns. Some have suggested the European Union, since it is a federation of many of the nations from the original Roman Empire. However, this group includes about thirty nations, far more than the ten horns.

Others suggest the G10 group of nations, while still others argue that the United Nations or a group like it will arise during the end times as a global governing body. While these attempts to identify the future ten horns have some correlations, it will unlikely be clear which specific group will be represented until the tribulation period.

The Antichrist is expected to be a formidable and feared dictator, and his coalition of ten kings may appear invincible. Yet Christ will decisively defeat this alliance of evil that is led by the ten-horned beast.

52. What Is the Significance of a Red Heifer in the Bible?

Recent headlines of red heifers in the US have been referred to as a sign of the end times.[8] These reports have led to many questions among some Christians. How could a red cow be an important part of Bible prophecy?

The red heifer plays a significant role in the purification rites outlined in the Mosaic law, as described in Numbers 19:1–10. This animal was a key part of the sacrificial system practiced by the Jews from the time of Moses through the period of the Jewish temple, up until the temple's destruction in AD 70.

Biblical prophecy indicates that a future Jewish temple will be constructed and later defiled by the Antichrist (Matthew 24:15). For the proper performance of temple sacrifices, the Mosaic law requires a red heifer.

Jewish rabbinical tradition holds that since the time of Moses, there have been nine red heifers sacrificed. No red heifers have been sacrificed since the destruction of the temple in the first century. The rabbi Maimonides (1135–1204) prophesied in the Parah Adumah that the Messiah would sacrifice the tenth red heifer.

Observant Jews also look forward to the fulfillment of Ezekiel 36:25–26, known as the Haftarah. This passage is interpreted as describing a divine act of purification, where God promises to cleanse the people from their sins by sprinkling them with clean water and providing them with a "new heart and…a new spirit." This promise of renewal and redemption

---

8 See, for example, Glenn Beck, "How Israel's Red Heifer Prophecy Explains What's Happening Right Now," YouTube, March 18, 2024, https://www.theblaze.com/shows.

aligns with the broader theme of redemption celebrated during Passover in Judaism.

Modern speculation about this idea of a red heifer has led to significant interest among prophecy voices, who see it as a key part of God's unfolding plans for a future Jewish temple and the fulfillment of prophecy. While such stories are interesting, they have arisen at least since the 1990s. Simply finding a red heifer does not mean a temple is about to be constructed or that Jesus is about to return. The animal is not some indication that the Antichrist is about to appear or that the mark of the beast is about to be implemented.

Biblical teachings about the red heifer are often viewed as foreshadowing Christ's sacrifice, highlighting parallel symbolic elements. The red heifer had to be flawless, similar to how the New Testament describes Christ as sinless. According to Numbers 19:2–3, the red heifer was sacrificed outside the camp, reflecting the crucifixion of Jesus, which occurred outside the walls of Jerusalem. Just as the ashes of the red heifer were used for purification from death, Christians believe that Jesus' sacrifice cleanses believers from the eternal effects and corruption of sin.

For Christians, Hebrews 4:14 identifies Christ as the Messiah and the great High Priest. Hebrews 9:11–14 elaborates on his role as high priest, describing him as the priest of "the good things to come." Christ entered the holy place with his own blood, making the sacrificial blood of goats, bulls, or red heifers obsolete. His redemptive work is complete and everlasting (4:13–14).

Jesus stated that the exact timing of his return is unknown (Mark 13:32). The next significant event in biblical prophecy is the rapture of believers (1 Corinthians 15:51–58; 1 Thessalonians 4:13–18), which could happen at any moment.

Observing signs that point to future prophetic events suggests that the fulfillment of biblical prophecy may be drawing near. This should encourage believers (1 Thessalonians 4:18) as they anticipate eternity with Christ. Such signs should also inspire us to live for the Lord and share our faith with those around us.

53. Who Are the Twenty-Four Elders in Revelation?

Revelation 4:4 describes twenty-four elders seated on twenty-four thrones before the Lord. The Bible does not explicitly identify these elders, but we can infer their nature based on several details.

First, the elders are believers in Christ. They are seen in heaven, wearing white garments that symbolize righteousness (Revelation 3:5, 18; 19:8). They also wear crowns, which are given to believers (1 Thessalonians 2:19; 2 Timothy 4:8; 1 Peter 5:4; Revelation 2:10). They also engage in worship of the Lord (Revelation 4:11).

Second, these elders are depicted as human males, not angels or other creatures. The text uses male terms for them and distinguishes them from angels, as seen in other parts of Revelation.

Given these characteristics, the twenty-four elders likely represent those who worship the Lord. They might symbolize the church and Israel or the twelve patriarchs and twelve apostles (Matthew 19:28).

One theory is that their number relates to the twenty-four divisions of priests mentioned in 1 Chronicles 24:1–5, suggesting that this "kingdom of priests" represents the church in heaven during the tribulation period. This interpretation addresses concerns about the representation of Israel during the tribulation, especially given that Israel had not yet widely accepted the Lord at that time.

It also avoids the issue of John, the apostle who had the vision, seeing himself among the elders without noting it. In other words, if the twenty-four elders included the apostles, John would have been looking at himself.

These elders also appear to be the same group mentioned in Revelation 7:11: "All the angels stood around the throne and the elders and the four living creatures, and fell on their faces before the throne and worshiped God."

They are mentioned again at the seventh trumpet: "The twenty-four elders who sat before God on their thrones fell on their faces and worshiped God" (Revelation 11:16). They are then mentioned a third time in Revelation 19:4: "The twenty-four elders and the four living creatures fell down and worshiped God who sat on the throne, saying, 'Amen! Alleluia!'" These beings are with the Lord in heaven throughout the tribulation period, likely representing the church that has been raptured before the judgments and enjoying the presence of the Lord.

In conclusion, although the Bible does not explicitly define the twenty-four elders, the evidence suggests they represent the church, depicted as those who are with the Lord during the tribulation while divine judgments unfold on earth. This aligns with the traditional view of elders as leaders of local churches (1 Timothy 3:1–7; Titus 1:5–9), illustrating God's people worshiping him after being raptured and before the tribulation.

54. Who Are the Two Witnesses in Revelation?

Revelation 11:3–12 introduces two significant figures known as the two witnesses. Who will these two men be and what will they do?

Three views are usually suggested about the identities of these two men. First, some have suggested that they will be Moses and Elijah returned to earth due to having similar miraculous abilities. Moses, alongside his brother Aaron, turned water into blood during the first plague (Exodus 7:14–25), a power mirrored in the actions of the two witnesses (Revelation 11:6). Elijah, who stopped rain through his prayers (1 Kings 17–18) and called fire down from heaven (2 Kings 1), shares parallels with the witnesses, who are also said to call down fire (Revelation 11:5). Furthermore, Moses and Elijah appeared with Jesus during the transfiguration, suggesting a possibility of their return (Matthew 17:3–4).

The second view is that these two witnesses represent Enoch and Elijah. This theory is based on the fact that Enoch and Elijah are the only two individuals in the Bible who were taken to heaven without experiencing death. Enoch was taken directly to heaven by God (Genesis 5:23–24; Hebrews 11:5), and Elijah was taken up in a chariot of fire (2 Kings 2:11). Since they did not die, it is thought that they might return to experience death and resurrection as the two witnesses.

The third perspective suggests that the two witnesses could be two future individuals who will be granted similar miraculous powers. This view allows for the possibility that the witnesses might not include Moses, Elijah, or Enoch but will be two new individuals empowered to perform miracles, such as turning water to blood and halting rain.

Their actions will serve to validate their message and lead many to faith in the Lord. Following their resurrection and ascension, a significant earthquake will occur, causing a portion of the city to collapse and resulting in numerous deaths, with many people turning to worship the true God (Revelation 11:13).

This third view appears most likely, as the Bible does not elsewhere describe a human returning to earth long-term after death. The parallels found in these two witnesses stand alongside numerous other parallels between activities in Revelation and Old Testament ideas. We should expect these similarities, but it does not require that the two witnesses will be Moses and Elijah.

These events are anticipated to occur near the midpoint of the seven-year tribulation described in Revelation. This period will be marked by severe judgment, the construction of a Jewish temple, and its desecration by the Antichrist, who will claim divinity. The two witnesses will play a crucial role in opposing this wicked ruler and directing people to the true God during these final, challenging times. Their efforts will take place alongside one hundred forty-four thousand Jewish evangelists and others who will share the news of the Messiah to those during the tribulation, indicating that the gospel will reach many even during these difficult days.

55. Who Are the 144,000 in Revelation?

The Bible mentions one hundred forty-four thousand people in the end times in Revelation 7:2–4. Who is this group of people, and what will they do? The text explains:

> I saw another angel ascending from the east, having the seal of the living God. And he cried with a loud voice to the four angels to whom it was granted to harm the earth and the sea, saying, "Do not harm the earth, the sea, or the trees till we have sealed the servants of our God on their foreheads." And I heard the number of those who were sealed. One hundred and forty-four thousand of all the tribes of the children of Israel were sealed.

The scene describes an angel with the seal of the living God who commands four other angels to refrain from damaging the earth, sea, or trees until the servants of God are marked on their foreheads. The text reveals that this group consists of one hundred forty-four thousand individuals from each of the twelve tribes of Israel.

According to Revelation 7:5–8, these one hundred forty-four thousand are identified as Jews, with twelve thousand from each tribe, and Scripture describes them as servants of God. This designation indicates they are believers who have accepted Jesus Christ as their Messiah. The seal on their foreheads could be a literal mark or a symbolic representation of their salvation, similar to the helmet of salvation Paul mentions in Ephesians 6:17. This mark is also in contrast with the mark of the beast.

The timing of their work is also explained. The angels are instructed not to cause harm until the sealing is complete. Since the destruction of the earth, sea, and trees occurs during the final three and a half years of the seven-year tribulation, the one hundred forty-four thousand will be active during the first half of this period, though their work might extend through the entire tribulation. Many interpreters view their role as fulfilling the prophecy in Matthew 24:14, which speaks of the gospel being preached worldwide before the end comes.

The existence of these one hundred forty-four thousand Jewish Christians during the tribulation period underscores the ongoing significance of Israel and the Jewish people. Despite the dangers they will face, many Jews will continue to live, and many will embrace Jesus as the Messiah.

It is also important to address the interpretation by Jehovah's Witnesses, who believe that the one hundred forty-four thousand represent a special group of their followers who will have a unique place in the afterlife. This interpretation is not supported by the biblical text, which identifies these individuals as Jewish believers in Jesus who serve on earth rather than in heaven.

Revelation also indicates that the one hundred forty-four thousand are not the only ones turning to God during this time. A multitude from various nations will worship God in heaven, highlighting that the one hundred forty-four thousand will play a crucial role in God's plan to spread the gospel in the last days.

56. Who Are the Tribulation Saints?

Some prophecy teachers discuss the idea of tribulation saints. The popular *Left Behind* series of books and movies even describes them as a Tribulation Force. What are tribulation saints? Is this really in the Bible?

Tribulation saints are individuals who will come to faith in Christ during the tribulation period. A seven-year tribulation with numerous judgments will follow the rapture. This period will culminate in the second coming of Jesus, initiating a one-thousand-year reign (Revelation 20:1–6).

Throughout this tribulation, one hundred forty-four thousand Jewish evangelists will spread the message of Jesus globally (7:1–7). Revelation 7:9 describes a vast multitude from every nation, tribe, and language standing before the throne and the Lamb, indicating that many will embrace faith in Christ during this period: "After these things I looked, and behold, a great multitude which no one could number, of all nations, tribes, peoples, and tongues, standing before the throne and before the Lamb, clothed with white robes, with palm branches in their hands."

Many of these tribulation saints will face martyrdom. Revelation 20:4 depicts the souls of those who were beheaded for their testimony of Jesus and who refused to worship the beast or accept its mark.

These martyrs will be resurrected at the start of the millennium and reign with Christ for a thousand years, according to this verse: "Then I saw the souls of those who had been beheaded for their witness to Jesus and for the word of God, who had not worshiped the beast or his image, and had not received his mark on their foreheads or on their hands. And they lived and reigned with Christ for a thousand years."

Revelation also mentions two witnesses who will prophesy, perform miracles, and spread Christ's message during the tribulation. They will also be martyred, but after three-and-a-half days, they will be resurrected and taken to heaven (11:3–12). Their powerful witness will likely contribute to the growth of Christianity during the tribulation.

Both Jews and gentiles will come to faith in Christ during these final days. While the severe judgments of the tribulation may seem daunting, one of their purposes is to lead more people to God.

Still, there is no need to wait for the tribulation to seek Christ. The difficult times the tribulation saints face can be avoided by believing in Jesus now to be prepared for Christ's rapture at any moment.

57. WHAT IS THE GREAT TRIBULATION?

In addition to a future seven-year tribulation period, the Bible also mentions a time called the great tribulation. Are these two events the same or different? What is this great tribulation?

The seven-year tribulation occurs between the rapture and the millennial kingdom, during which the Antichrist will rise to power through Satan's influence. In Daniel 9:24–27, Daniel's prophecy outlines a period of seventy "weeks" (each week being seven years, totaling 490 years), during which sin will end and righteousness will prevail.

The prophecy begins with the decree to restore Jerusalem, issued around 445 BC by King Artaxerxes of Persia (Nehemiah

2). The arrival and subsequent crucifixion of the Messiah would occur after sixty-nine weeks, marked by Christ's triumphal entry and crucifixion.

The final "week" of years is the tribulation period. It is our understanding that the church age is not part of these seventy weeks. The next event will be the rapture of the church, which can happen at any moment (1 Thessalonians 4:13–18). This will be followed by Daniel's seventieth week, known as the tribulation, detailed in Daniel 9:26–27.

The tribulation is often discussed in two parts, dividing it in half by three-and-a-half years. The final half is referred to by Jesus as the great tribulation. Matthew 24:21 says, "Then there will be great tribulation, such as has not been since the beginning of the world until this time, no, nor ever shall be."

This great tribulation will begin with the rise of the Antichrist's power, last for forty-two months (Revelation 13:5), and conclude with Christ's second coming (Matthew 24:29–30). The Antichrist will begin by confirming a seven-year peace treaty with Israel and its adversaries (Daniel 9:26–27). At the midpoint, the Antichrist will commit blasphemy, desecrate the temple, persecute believers, and assume global dominance (Revelation 13:1–10). According to Daniel, he will halt sacrifices and offerings, and according to Revelation, there will be widespread imprisonment and martyrdom of believers under his rule.

Israel will endure unprecedented suffering during this time (Daniel 12:1; Jeremiah 30:7). The great tribulation will also represent a period of divine judgment on the earth. While the Antichrist persecutes believers and Jews, God will punish those who have rejected him. Revelation 13–19 details these judgments, with 14:9–11 warning of eternal condemnation for those who worship the beast.

As the end approaches, the Euphrates River will dry up, enabling eastern armies to advance toward Israel (Revelation 16:12–16). The battle of Armageddon will ensue, with nations clashing against the Antichrist's forces, culminating in a final confrontation involving Jesus and heavenly armies (19:11–21). The Antichrist and his false prophet will be cast alive into the lake of fire, and Satan will be bound and imprisoned for a thousand years (20:3).

The great tribulation will be a time of intense turmoil and suffering. The description of this difficult future time is a powerful reminder of the need to believe in Jesus.

58. WILL THE HOLY SPIRIT STILL OPERATE ON THE EARTH DURING THE TRIBULATION?

Some have claimed that the Holy Spirit will no longer operate during the future seven-year tribulation period. What does the Bible teach about this issue?

The basis for this idea comes from 2 Thessalonians 2:7, which states, "The mystery of lawlessness is already at work; only He who now restrains will do so until He is taken out of the way." This passage is interpreted to mean that the Antichrist will gain power because the Holy Spirit will cease to restrain evil during that time. However, this interpretation does not state that the Holy Spirit will be completely absent from the world during the tribulation.

The role of the Holy Spirit in salvation and spiritual growth is important for all believers, including those who will come to faith during the tribulation. Believers are spiritually reborn through the Holy Spirit, and this spiritual rebirth is necessary for entering the kingdom of God. Jesus said in John 3:5, "Most assuredly, I say to you, unless one is born of water and the Spirit, he cannot enter the kingdom of God."

The Spirit is responsible for regenerating and preparing individual souls for salvation (Titus 3:5). The Holy Spirit is also essential for ongoing growth or sanctification: "God from the beginning chose you for salvation through sanctification by the Spirit and belief in the truth," Paul teaches in 2 Thessalonians 2:13. Since the Holy Spirit is fundamental to these processes, his presence is crucial, even during the tribulation. The fact that people will be saved during this period confirms that the Holy Spirit must still be at work.

Revelation provides clear evidence that individuals will come to faith during the tribulation. In a vision recorded in Revelation 7:9, the apostle John saw "a great multitude which no one could number, of all nations, tribes, peoples, and tongues, standing before the throne and before the Lamb, clothed with white robes, with palm branches in their hands," praising God for their salvation. An elder then explained to John that these people are coming "out of the great tribulation," having "washed their robes and made them white in the blood of the Lamb" (vv. 13–14).

This vision offers reassurance that the Holy Spirit will continue to operate during the tribulation period. There may be some differences since believers from the church age will be in heaven, but God's Spirit will provide ongoing help in salvation to many during the difficult days of the tribulation. We can also be encouraged that many Jews and non-Jews will believe during the tribulation, extending God's grace even to those who do not go to be with the Lord at the rapture.

SECTION 7

GOD'S FUTURE JUDGMENTS

59. What Are the Future Judgments Found in Revelation?

The book of Revelation describes three sets of seven judgments that will unfold during the future tribulation period. They will include the seven seals, trumpets, and bowls (also called vials in some translations). While some have attempted to explain portions of these judgments as already taking place, the evidence points to a future fulfillment for these events.

The judgments are divided into three series: seals, trumpets, and bowls, introduced in chapters 6, 8, and 15 of Revelation. Each series consists of seven distinct acts of destruction. The number seven often symbolizes completeness or perfection in the Bible, and the three sets of judgments might reflect the completeness of God's wrath and/or the triune nature of God.

The seal judgments are first revealed in Revelation 5:1–5. In this passage, God the Father, signifying authority, holds a scroll sealed with seven seals. The scroll, written on both sides, is typical of ancient contracts. Jesus Christ, depicted as the

Lion of Judah, is found worthy to open the scroll and its seals, indicating his authority to reclaim and restore the earth.

The first six seal judgments, detailed in Revelation 6, are (1) the emergence of the Antichrist, (2) the start of wars and loss of peace, (3) famine, (4) death resulting from war and famine, (5) the persecution of believers, and (6) a massive earthquake and other disasters. Jesus also described these judgments in Matthew 24.

The seventh seal, opened in Revelation 8–9, introduces the trumpet judgments: (1) the destruction of a third of the earth's vegetation, (2) the death of a third of all sea creatures and the destruction of ships, (3) the pollution of all waters and widespread death, (4) the darkening of a third of the sun, moon, and stars, (5) the release of locusts or demons to torment people, and (6) the release of the four bound demons, who will kill a third of all people.

The seventh trumpet signals Christ's imminent return and precedes the bowl judgments: (1) painful sores on those with the mark of the beast, (2) the death of all sea life, (3) the poisoning of all fresh waters, (4) intense heat from the sun, (5) darkness over the Antichrist's kingdom, (6) the drying up of the Euphrates, and (7) a massive earthquake, the collapse of cities, and a great hailstorm.

God's promises of future wrath will one day cause unthinkable disasters on the earth. These warnings of upcoming judgment should serve as a warning to believe in Jesus today and to share him with others to avoid this terrible series of events.

60. What Are the Seven Seals in Revelation?

During the end times, the seven-year tribulation will include three sets of seven judgments (see the previous question). The seven seals will represent the first of these three series of divine judgments as outlined in Revelation 6:1–17 and 8:1–5.

In John's vision, he first saw an angel seeking someone worthy to open a scroll that would initiate these judgments. John was distressed when no one was found worthy to open the scroll, as described in Revelation 5:4. However, an elder reassured him that "the Lion of the tribe of Judah, the Root of David, has prevailed" and was worthy to open the scroll and its seven seals (5:5).

John then saw Jesus, depicted as a lamb that appeared slain, taking the scroll from God's right hand (vv. 6–7). This symbolizes Jesus' unique role in executing the world's judgment. The four living creatures and twenty-four elders worshiped Jesus and acknowledged his authority (vv. 8–14). As Jesus broke the first seal, the first judgment was revealed.

The first four seals introduce the four horsemen of the Apocalypse: "I looked, and behold, a white horse. He who sat on it had a bow; and a crown was given to him, and he went out conquering and to conquer" (6:2). This seal releases the Antichrist, symbolized by a white horse and crown that suggest his deceptive promotion of peace and power. The bow indicates his intent to deceive and conquer, contrasting with the white horse imagery used for Jesus' second coming in 19:11, where Jesus wields a sword for justice.

The second seal ushers in a period of widespread war, surpassing any previous conflicts in intensity: "Another horse, fiery red, went out. And it was granted to the one who sat on it to take peace from the earth, and that people should kill one another; and there was given to him a great sword" (6:4).

The third seal reveals a severe famine, leading to significant hardship and low yields despite extensive effort: "When He opened the third seal, I heard the third living creature say, 'Come and see.' So I looked, and behold, a black horse, and he who sat on it had a pair of scales in his hand" (v. 5).

The fourth seal brings death that will claim a quarter of the world's population through war, famine, and wild beasts: "I looked, and behold, a pale horse. And the name of him who sat on it was Death, and Hades followed with him. And power was given to them over a fourth of the earth, to kill with sword, with hunger, with death, and by the beasts of the earth" (v. 8).

The fifth seal reveals the souls of martyrs asking when they will be avenged. God provides them with white robes and promises retribution once the full number of martyrs is reached: "When He opened the fifth seal, I saw under the altar the souls of those who had been slain for the word of God and for the testimony which they held" (v. 9).

The sixth seal triggers a massive earthquake, affecting celestial bodies and causing people to hide from God's wrath in fear: "I looked when He opened the sixth seal, and behold, there was a great earthquake; and the sun became black as sackcloth of hair, and the moon became like blood. And the stars of heaven fell to the earth, as a fig tree drops its late figs when it is shaken by a mighty wind" (vv. 12–13).

After the sixth seal, an angel marks one hundred forty-four thousand people to protect them during the ensuing judgments and commissions them to spread the gospel (Revelation 7). This is confirmed by a vision of believers from every nation worshiping God in heaven, having come out of the tribulation.

The seventh seal precedes the second series of judgments, the seven trumpets, which are even more severe as the end approaches: "When He opened the seventh seal, there was silence in heaven for about half an hour" (8:1).

Despite these opportunities for repentance, many will reject God and curse him for his judgments. The opening of the seventh seal will begin the unfolding of the seven trumpets, in which even more difficult judgments will be unveiled.

61. What Are the Seven Trumpets in Revelation?

During the seven-year tribulation, God will execute his judgment on a sinful world and issue a final call for repentance and worship. Revelation contains a vision from God given to John, detailing three sets of seven: the seven seals, seven trumpets, and seven bowls. The second set, the seven trumpets, is covered in Revelation 8:6–9:21 and 11:15–19.

John's vision reveals seven angels holding trumpets and standing before God. An additional angel offers incense mixed with the prayers of the faithful at the altar and then casts fire from the altar onto the earth (8:2–5). Following this, the first angel blows his trumpet.

The first trumpet (v. 7) will bring hail and fiery blood to the earth, destroying one-third of the trees and grass. This judgment is similar to the seventh plague that God brought upon ancient Egypt (Exodus 9:13–35).

The second trumpet (Revelation 8:8) will send a fiery mountain into the sea, killing a third of sea life and destroying a third of the ships on the water.

The third trumpet (8:10) introduces a star named Wormwood, which will poison one-third of the earth's waters, making them bitter and causing numerous deaths.

The fourth trumpet (v. 12) will reduce light by one-third, causing partial darkness both day and night.

The fifth through seventh trumpets are termed the "three woes," as an eagle warns of the intense suffering ahead (v. 13). The fifth trumpet (9:5) will release a fallen angel who opens the Abyss, unleashing locusts led by Abaddon. These locusts, described with various disturbing features, torment for five months those without God's seal. Interpretations vary, with some suggesting these creatures are symbolic of some form of future technology.

The sixth trumpet (9:15) will release four bound angels at the Euphrates River to lead a vast army that kills one-third of humanity. These angels will ride horses and wear breastplates of red, blue, and yellow to represent the plagues they inflict. The plagues will include fire, smoke, and sulfur.

The seventh trumpet (11:15) will reveal the heavenly temple and the ark of the covenant. The heavens will celebrate, knowing that Jesus will soon defeat Satan and establish his eternal kingdom.

Despite these severe judgments, many will not repent and will persist in their sinfulness, similar to how the Egyptians hardened their hearts against Moses' plagues. These events will precede the sounding of the seventh trumpet and the commencement of the final series of judgments, the seven bowls or vial judgments.

62. What Are the Seven Bowls or Vials in Revelation?

In the book of Revelation, John recounts a vision from God about the end times, which includes a seven-year tribulation. During this period, God will unleash his wrath as judgment for the world's sins and as a final opportunity for humanity to repent and worship him. This judgment is depicted in three series of seven: the seven seals, seven trumpets, and seven bowls. The seven bowls or vials of God's wrath are detailed in Revelation 16:1–21.

John witnessed seven angels holding seven plagues, described as the final outpouring of God's wrath (Revelation 15:1). A heavenly voice instructs these angels to pour out their bowls of wrath upon the earth: "Then I heard a loud voice from the temple saying to the seven angels, 'Go and pour out the bowls of the wrath of God on the earth'" (16:1).

The first bowl will cause painful sores to erupt on those who have aligned themselves with the Antichrist, leaving God's followers unaffected. "The first went and poured out his bowl upon the earth, and a foul and loathsome sore came upon the men who had the mark of the beast and those who worshiped his image" (16:2).

The second bowl will turn the sea into blood, killing all remaining sea life (the second trumpet already destroyed a third of the sea's creatures). "Then the second angel poured out his bowl on the sea, and it became blood as of a dead man; and every living creature in the sea died" (v. 3).

The third bowl will transform all sources of fresh water into blood. The angel announces that this judgment is just, as those who shed the blood of believers will now drink blood themselves (v. 4).

The fourth bowl will cause the sun to scorch people with intense heat. Despite their suffering, the people will curse God but refuse to repent and give him glory (v. 8).

The fifth bowl will plunge the Antichrist's kingdom into profound darkness, causing people to suffer so greatly that they gnaw their tongues in pain. The people will continue to curse God rather than repent (v. 10).

The sixth bowl will dry up the Euphrates River to make way for the kings from the east, facilitating the final confrontation at Armageddon where Satan, the Antichrist, and the false prophet will gather to wage war against Jesus (v. 12).

The seventh bowl will announce the completion of God's judgment. It will trigger a catastrophic earthquake, splitting Jerusalem into three parts, causing the collapse of cities, and making mountains and islands disappear. Giant hailstones, weighing about a hundred pounds each, will fall on the people, who continue to curse God without repenting.

Following the seventh bowl, an angel revealed to John the judgment upon Babylon (Revelation 17–18). While the inhabitants of the earth mourn Babylon's fall, heaven will rejoice, recognizing God's justice in condemning her for deceiving nations and shedding the blood of prophets and saints.

After the judgment of Babylon, John saw a vision of a white horse with a rider called Faithful and True, who judges and makes war in righteousness. This rider is Jesus, coming to defeat Satan and establish his eternal kingdom on earth (19:11).

63. What Is the Importance of the Eastern Gate of Jerusalem in the End Times?

Some teach that Jesus will return through the Eastern Gate of Jerusalem in the end times. Is this an accurate interpretation of the Bible prophecies?

The Eastern Gate of Jerusalem, also known as the Golden Gate or Beautiful Gate, faces the Mount of Olives across the Kidron Valley and is notable for being completely sealed. This gate is the oldest gate in Jerusalem. It provides the most direct access to the Temple Mount, where the Jewish temple once stood. Jesus entered Jerusalem from the Mount of Olives through a gate in the same location as the current Eastern Gate.

In Ezekiel, there are several references to an eastern gate. Ezekiel describes the Lord's glory leaving the temple through the Eastern Gate and then returning through the same gate (Ezekiel 10:18–19; 11:23; 43:1–5).

Ezekiel 44:1–2 says that the gate is to remain shut because it has been used by the Lord. Ezekiel 46:12 says that the gate will be opened for the prince to offer sacrifices but will close afterward.

Some interpret these passages as referring to Jesus. They see the glory of the Lord entering the temple as symbolic of Jesus' triumphal entry into Jerusalem, and they view the sealing of the gate as a foretelling of the historical sealing of the gate in Jewish history. The prince is viewed as a reference to

Christ's future return, when he will reenter Jerusalem through the Eastern Gate.

However, this interpretation is unlikely. Ezekiel's "gate facing east" is described as part of the temple court, not the city gate. In addition, the current Eastern Gate was built long after Jesus' time. The original gate, which Jesus would have used, is located underground beneath the existing gate. The temple and the city described in Ezekiel's vision are different from the Jerusalem of Jesus' time, with the future temple being much larger.

The prince mentioned in Ezekiel 46 is not identified as the Messiah but as an overseer of the millennial kingdom who operates under Christ's authority. This prince must make sin offerings, indicating he is a human with a sinful nature, unlike Jesus who is sinless.

Ezekiel's eastern gate is part of the future millennial temple. In his prophecy, the departure and return of the Lord's glory symbolize the first temple's destruction and the future temple's restoration. The closed eastern gate signifies the permanence of the Lord's presence in the future temple.

Yes, Jesus will return at the end of the tribulation at his second coming (Revelation 19). He will also reign from a new millennial temple in Jerusalem. However, the prediction of the Eastern Gate is part of the future millennial period rather than a reference to where Jesus will first return to earth.

64. What Are the Differences Between the Trumpet in 1 Thessalonians 4 and the Seven Trumpets in Revelation?

Trumpets are mentioned in the passages about the rapture in 1 Corinthians 15:52 and 1 Thessalonians 4:16. How do they relate to the seven trumpets in Revelation?

Those who interpret these passages as referring to the same trumpet often argue that the rapture occurs mid-tribulation, around the three-and-a-half-year mark of the seven-year tribulation. But if the trumpet in Revelation 11:15 is considered distinct from those in 1 Corinthians 15 and 1 Thessalonians 4, this suggests a pretribulation rapture. This is the more likely scenario.

Revelation 11:15 describes a trumpet sounding at the midpoint of the tribulation, marking the end of the ministry of the two witnesses and the conclusion of the second woe: "Then the seventh angel sounded: And there were loud voices in heaven, saying, 'The kingdoms of this world have become the kingdoms of our Lord and of His Christ, and He shall reign forever and ever!'" This event associates the trumpet with the tribulation period.

In contrast, 1 Corinthians 15:51–52 speaks of a trumpet that signals the transformation of believers, both the dead and the living, at a moment not tied to any specific time frame. This trumpet heralds the resurrection and transformation of believers rather than a specific judgment or event within the tribulation.

First Thessalonians 4:16–17 describes the same event as 1 Corinthians 15, where the Lord descends from heaven with a trumpet sound to gather his followers. This passage provides details unique from those found in Revelation 11. Some of the differences include the Lord's descent from heaven, which is not described in Revelation 11 but is mentioned in Revelation 19 during the second coming.

Revelation includes seven distinct trumpets, each associated with different judgments throughout the tribulation. These judgments are separate from the rapture described in 1 Corinthians and 1 Thessalonians, which will occur before the tribulation.

Thus, the trumpets associated with the rapture passages in 1 Corinthians 15 and 1 Thessalonians 4 are not the same as the seven trumpets in Revelation. There are too many differences in the timing and details surrounding these two different periods, with the trumpet judgments of Revelation unfolding later as God brings judgment upon the earth before his second coming.

65. What Is the Battle of Armageddon?

Revelation predicts a coming battle, called the battle of Armageddon, where Jesus will return in judgment against his enemies. Revelation 16:15–16 associates the coming fulfillment of this event during the sixth bowl judgment: "'Behold, I am coming as a thief. Blessed is he who watches, and keeps his garments, lest he walk naked and they see his shame.' And they gathered them together to the place called in Hebrew, Armageddon."

This passage is part of the bowl judgments during the great tribulation, which depict the escalation of God's wrath against an unbelieving world. The final culmination of these judgments involves gathering the forces of the Antichrist and all other armies into a single location for their ultimate destruction by God.

John's vision begins with the drying up of the Euphrates River, which historically marked the boundary between the east and west. By drying up this river, God will remove a significant obstacle, facilitating the movement of an eastern army toward Israel. This action will prepare the way for a massive invasion led by the Antichrist.

Three demonic spirits emerging from the dragon (Satan), the beast (Antichrist), and the false prophet deceive the kings of the world into gathering for battle against God. The armies, convinced by these evil entities and their miracles, converge on Israel, aiming to fight against God himself: "I saw the beast, the kings of the earth, and their armies, gathered together to make war against Him who sat on the horse and against His army" (Revelation 19:19).

The location of this future epic battle is likely the hilly region surrounding the Plain of Megiddo, about sixty miles north of Jerusalem. At this site, all the gathered armies will face God's judgment in the second coming of Christ. The armies will be defeated: "These will make war with the Lamb, and the Lamb will overcome them, for He is Lord of lords and King of kings; and those who are with Him are called, chosen, and faithful" (17:14).

The conclusion of this battle is the defeat of the Antichrist and his forces: "Then the beast was captured, and with him the false prophet who worked signs in his presence, by which he deceived those who received the mark of the beast and those who worshiped his image. These two were cast alive into the lake of fire burning with brimstone. And the rest were killed with the sword which proceeded from the mouth of Him who sat on the horse. And all the birds were filled with their flesh" (19:20–21).

Some prophecy teachers describe this future battle as a campaign due to its long buildup. The conclusion of this conflict will result in Jesus beginning his millennial reign while his enemies are bound in the lake of fire.

66. What is Wormwood in Revelation?

In Revelation, wormwood is introduced as part of the judgment during the tribulation period, specifically linked to the third trumpet (Revelation 8:10–11). What is wormwood, and why is it important?

Wormwood is a plant native to North Africa and parts of the Mediterranean. It has white or greenish-silver stems and has been used for hundreds of years for various purposes. Historically, it has been known for its bitter flavor, which is the association of the plant in Revelation and other prophetic Bible passages.

Revelation 8:10–11 describes this event: "The third angel sounded: And a great star fell from heaven, burning like a torch, and it fell on a third of the rivers and on the springs of water. The name of the star is Wormwood. A third of the waters became wormwood, and many men died from the water, because it was made bitter." In this passage, wormwood symbolizes a star that falls from heaven, causing a third of the earth's freshwater sources to become contaminated and lethal.

The term "wormwood" has significant connotations from the Old Testament, where it is frequently associated with bitterness and death. Proverbs 5:3–5 warns, "The lips of an immoral woman drip honey, and her mouth is smoother than oil; but in the end she is bitter as wormwood, sharp as a two-edged sword. Her feet go down to death, her steps lay hold of hell."

Lamentations 3:15 also reflects this association: "He has filled me with bitterness; he has made me drink wormwood," and 3:19 as well says, "Remember my affliction and roaming, the wormwood and the gall."

The prophet Amos also noted wormwood on two occasions. Amos 5:7 says, "You who turn justice to wormwood, and lay righteousness to rest in the earth!" Amos 6:12 states, "Do horses run on rocks? Does one plow there with oxen? Yet you have turned justice into gall, and the fruit of righteousness into wormwood."

The original readers of Revelation would have understood wormwood to signify something extremely bitter or harmful, as demonstrated by the text wherein many die from the poisoned waters—one of a series of disastrous judgments that lead up to the second coming of Christ.

67. Who is Apollyon in Revelation?

In Revelation 9:11, John records the name Apollyon: "They had as king over them the angel of the bottomless pit, whose name in Hebrew is Abaddon, but in Greek he has the name

Apollyon." The term *abaddon* in Hebrew translates to "place of destruction," while *apollyon* in Greek means "destroyer."

In the context of Revelation 9, John described a series of trumpet blasts marking the unfolding judgments during the end times. When the fifth angel sounds his trumpet, the Abyss, a vast smoking chasm, opens, releasing a swarm of demonic "locusts" in verse 3: "Then out of the smoke locusts came upon the earth. And to them was given power, as the scorpions of the earth have power."

These locusts will be empowered to torment everyone who does not have God's seal on their foreheads: "They were commanded not to harm the grass of the earth, or any green thing, or any tree, but only those men who do not have the seal of God on their foreheads" (v. 4). Their suffering will be so severe that people will long for death: "In those days men will seek death and will not find it; they will desire to die, and death will flee from them" (v. 6). Apollyon will preside over the Abyss and command these tormenting locusts.

Though Apollyon is sometimes equated with Satan, Scripture seems to differentiate them. Satan is mentioned later in Revelation as being bound for a thousand years (Revelation 20:1–3), released to cause further chaos (vv. 1–8), and ultimately facing his eternal judgment (v. 10). It is more likely that Apollyon represents one of Satan's demons.

In John Bunyan's classic book *The Pilgrim's Progress*, Christian battles a demonic entity named Apollyon. True to its name, Apollyon nearly defeats Christian, who fends off the monster. Bunyan's fictional account draws inspiration from the Apollyon in Revelation, who represents a genuine force of torment and destruction destined to play a role in divine judgment.

Apollyon is one of two fallen angels described by name in the Bible. Lucifer was once a radiant and exalted angel but became the first to defy God. His ambition to usurp God's position led him to rebellion, resulting in his expulsion from heaven along with his followers (Isaiah 14:12–18; Luke 10:18). After his fall, Lucifer was transformed into a malevolent entity known as Satan or the devil, who stands in opposition to God and seeks to deceive God's image bearers (John 10:10).

In Revelation 9:11, Apollyon is introduced as the leader of a demonic army during the final days. John described him in violent terms, saying that he will serve as one of the chief evil spirits opposing God and his people in the last days.

68. Who Are Gog and Magog?

Gog and Magog are two important names in the final predictions described in Revelation 20. Who are these people or groups?

The names Gog and Magog in the Bible refer to different entities depending on the context. Originally, Magog was one of Noah's grandsons, a descendant of Japheth, whose lineage is believed to have settled in northern regions such as Europe and Northern Asia (Genesis 10). Over time, these names evolved to represent hostile nations opposed to Israel.

Ezekiel prophesied that Gog and Magog will be adversarial forces that will attack Israel during a time of peace, likely during the first half of the tribulation when Israel has a covenant with the Antichrist (Ezekiel 38:14–15; Daniel 9:27). This prophecy describes a powerful nation from the north invading Israel, but God will decisively defeat them to demonstrate his protection over the Jewish people (Ezekiel 39:1–7).

The term "Gog and Magog" in Revelation refers to a different scenario that will occur after the one-thousand-year millennial kingdom. In this context, they symbolize a coalition of nations from around the world stirred by Satan to rebel against God. Revelation 20:7–8 says, "Now when the thousand years have expired, Satan will be released from his prison and will go out to deceive the nations which are in the four corners of the earth, Gog and Magog, to gather them together to battle, whose number is as the sand of the sea."

Because Gog and Magog are mentioned in these verses alongside God's enemies from the four corners of the earth, some argue that they represent those worldwide who oppose Jesus and his millennial kingdom. These nations will surround the city of God, but they will be swiftly defeated. Satan will be cast into the lake of fire just before the great white throne judgment (vv. 7–11).

While interpretations vary, some scholars have speculated that Gog and Magog might refer to Russia and its ruler due to geographical and historical connections. In Ezekiel 38, Gog is noted as the ruler of Magog. The land of Magog was historically the region north of the Black Sea, which includes parts of modern-day Russia. Other historical sources have suggested Magog refers to parts of Asia Minor, located in modern Turkey.

The similarities between the two biblical battles—such as the antagonists' hostile intentions, their coalition of forces, and their ultimate defeat by God—suggest that the Revelation account might echo the earlier prophecy in Ezekiel. This resemblance might be intentional, highlighting recurring themes of divine intervention and judgment.

69. WHO ARE THE FOUR HORSEMEN OF THE END TIMES?

The four horsemen have been the focus of many aspects of popular culture. From the television shows *Sleepy Hollow* and *Supernatural* to a popular Metallica song and the video game *Call of Duty*, the idea has fascinated people for many years. Who are the four horsemen in Revelation?

The concept of the "four horsemen of the Apocalypse" originates in Revelation 6. John describes a series of catastrophic judgments that will occur during the tribulation period. These judgments are divided into three groups: the seal judgments, the trumpet judgments, and the bowl judgments. Collectively, they are referred to as the "great tribulation," a term used by Jesus in Matthew 24 to describe a period of unprecedented suffering: "Then there will be great tribulation, such as has not been since the beginning of the world until this time, no, nor ever shall be" (v. 21).

The first set of judgments, the seal judgments, is introduced in Revelation 5, where John sees a scroll sealed with seven seals. This scroll symbolizes the title deed to the earth, which belongs to Christ. Only Jesus is worthy to open it, and each broken seal initiates a corresponding judgment as he reclaims what has been lost to Satan and the world.

The first four seals reveal four horsemen, each with a distinct role. The first horseman rides a white horse: "I looked, and behold, a white horse. He who sat on it had a bow; and a crown was given to him, and he went out conquering and to conquer" (Revelation 6:2). He is often interpreted as representing the Antichrist, who brings a deceptive peace to the world.

This peace, however, is short-lived and ultimately false. The rider's white horse and crown symbolize conquest and authority, while his having a bow but no arrows suggests that his initial victories are achieved through diplomacy rather than force.

The second horseman rides a red horse and symbolizes the outbreak of widespread war: "Another horse, fiery red, went out. And it was granted to the one who sat on it to take peace from the earth, and that people should kill one another; and there was given to him a great sword" (v. 4). This rider is granted the authority to remove peace from the earth, leading to violence and bloodshed. The "great sword" he wields signifies the intense and destructive nature of the conflicts that will ensue.

The third horseman rides a black horse and represents famine: "I looked, and behold, a black horse, and he who sat on it had a pair of scales in his hand" (v. 5). He carries a set of scales, indicating the severe scarcity of food. The announcement of high prices for basic commodities (v. 6) highlights the dire conditions of widespread hunger, with food becoming prohibitively expensive and scarce.

The fourth horseman rides a pale horse, and his name is Death. He is accompanied by Hades: "I looked, and behold, a pale horse. And the name of him who sat on it was Death, and Hades followed with him. And power was given to them over a fourth of the earth, to kill with sword, with hunger, with death, and by the beasts of the earth" (v. 8). This rider signifies the culmination of the preceding judgments, bringing death through war, famine, pestilence, and wild beasts. The pale color of the horse reflects the appearance of death and decay.

Together, these four horsemen will bring about immense suffering, affecting a quarter of the earth's population. This period of tribulation, described as the most intense ever, is only the beginning of further divine judgments that will follow.

70. What Is the War in Heaven in Revelation 12?

In Revelation 12:7–12, John describes a heavenly battle wherein Satan and his followers are cast out of heaven. When does this take place? What is this war in heaven?

Some identify this war with the book of Job. In Job 1 and 2, Satan has access to the heavenly realm, where he presents himself before the Lord. This indicates that the battle described in Revelation 12 must occur after the time of Job.

In Zechariah 3, the prophet recounts an incident where Satan appears before God to accuse Joshua, further suggesting that Satan had access to heaven during the Old Testament period. Verses 1–2 note: "He showed me Joshua the high priest standing before the Angel of the Lord, and Satan standing at his right hand to oppose him. And the Lord said to Satan, 'The Lord rebuke you, Satan! The Lord who has chosen Jerusalem rebuke you! Is this not a brand plucked from the fire?'"

In the New Testament, Ephesians 6:11–12 describes spiritual conflict involving Satan and his forces: "Put on the whole armor of God, that you may be able to stand against the wiles of the devil. For we do not wrestle against flesh and blood, but against principalities, against powers, against the rulers of the darkness of this age, against spiritual hosts of wickedness in the heavenly places."

Written around AD 60–62, this epistle shows that Satan was still considered to have access to the heavenly realm at that time, which was roughly thirty to thirty-five years before Revelation was written. These passages collectively suggest that the event in Revelation 12, where Satan is expelled from heaven, is a future occurrence.

Revelation 12:6 indicates that this expulsion will occur around the midpoint of the tribulation period: "Then the woman fled into the wilderness, where she has a place prepared by God, that they should feed her there one thousand two hundred and sixty days." This will lead to a period of intense persecution for God's people as Satan is described as coming down with "great wrath" because his time is short (v. 12).

Regarding Satan's original fall, it certainly happened before he tempted Adam and Eve in the garden of Eden but after the creation of angelic beings. Ezekiel 28:11–19 and Isaiah 14 discuss this event. Ezekiel 28 transitions from addressing the king of Tyre to proclaiming against the supernatural figure of Lucifer, who in his pride sought to surpass God and ultimately led to his fall.

Satan was initially a powerful angel who rebelled against God and was cast from his exalted position. Though he was removed from his heavenly role, he has been permitted limited access to heaven and has been active on earth. He will be completely expelled from heaven at the midpoint of the tribulation, after which he will intensify his attacks against God's people until his ultimate defeat at Armageddon and his final judgment (Revelation 19–20).

SECTION 8

THE SECOND COMING AND THE MILLENNIAL KINGDOM

71. WHAT IS THE SECOND COMING AND WHAT WILL HAPPEN AT THAT TIME?

What is the second coming? Many have combined this event with the rapture and misunderstand the order of activities surrounding this important end-time event.

The second coming of Jesus refers to the time when Christ will return to earth, defeat his enemies, and establish his reign as the King of kings. Jesus described this event in Matthew 24:30: "Then the sign of the Son of Man will appear in heaven, and then all the tribes of the earth will mourn, and they will see the Son of Man coming on the clouds of heaven with power and great glory."

In Revelation 19:11–16, John depicts Jesus as a powerful warrior. Verses 11–13 describe him:

> Now I saw heaven opened, and behold, a white horse. And He who sat on him was called Faithful and True, and in righteousness He judges and makes war. His eyes were like a flame of fire, and on His head were many crowns. He had a name written that no one knew except Himself. He was clothed with a robe dipped in blood, and His name is called The Word of God.

Initially, the concept of Jesus' second coming was unclear to both Jews and early Christians. While they were familiar with the prophecies of a suffering servant (Isaiah 53) and a conquering king (Isaiah 7:14; 9:6–7), they did not realize that these roles would unfold at different times.

The people welcomed Jesus into Jerusalem with palms and cloaks, expecting him to deliver them from Roman occupation. Even after his resurrection, the disciples struggled to grasp that his departure was necessary before his return. The angels clarified this to the disciples after Jesus' ascension, saying, "Men of Galilee, why do you stand gazing up into heaven? This same Jesus, who was taken up from you into heaven, will so come in like manner as you saw Him go into heaven" (Acts 1:11).

Today, there is often confusion between the second coming of Christ and the rapture of the church. The rapture is described in 1 Thessalonians 4:16–17: "The Lord Himself will descend from heaven with a shout, with the voice of an archangel, and with the trumpet of God. And the dead in Christ will rise first. Then we who are alive and remain shall be caught up together with them in the clouds to meet the Lord in the air. And thus we shall always be with the Lord." During the rapture, Jesus will meet his followers in the air but will not return to earth.

In contrast, Zechariah 14:4 prophesies that Jesus will "stand on the Mount of Olives" upon his return. His second coming will fulfill prophecies, defeat his enemies (Zechariah 12:1–9; Revelation 19:15–16), and establish his reign as King (Isaiah 11). The second coming will take place at the end of the seven-year tribulation. The promise of his return is meant to offer encouragement (Titus 2:13) and to remind us that God will one day fulfill all of his promises.

72. What Does It Mean That Jesus Will Return on Clouds?

Many people claim that Jesus will come back on clouds. Is this true? What does the Bible teach about the way Christ will return?

In the opening of Revelation, John depicts the return of Jesus with the following words: "Behold, He is coming with clouds, and every eye will see Him, even they who pierced Him. And all the tribes of the earth will mourn because of Him. Even so, Amen" (Revelation 1:7).

The phrase "with clouds" is likely literal. Attempts to assign alternative meanings to this description seem unnecessary. Jesus also addressed this imagery during his earthly ministry.

In the Old Testament, the day of the Lord was sometimes associated with a day of clouds. For example, Ezekiel 30:3 predicts, "For the day is near, even the day of the Lord is near; it will be a day of clouds, the time of the Gentiles." Zephaniah 1:15 adds that this day will be "a day of clouds and thick darkness."

Jesus told his followers in Matthew 24:30, "Then the sign of the Son of Man will appear in heaven, and then all the tribes of the earth will mourn, and they will see the Son of Man coming on the clouds of heaven with power and great glory." Jesus predicted his return on clouds at his second coming. Revelation 19 says that this will occur when he comes in power at the end of the seven-year tribulation to defeat his enemies.

Mark 13:24–26 notes a similar prediction: "In those days, after that tribulation, the sun will be darkened, and the moon will not give its light; the stars of heaven will fall, and the powers in the heavens will be shaken. Then they will see the Son of Man coming in the clouds with great power and glory."

Before his crucifixion, Jesus told the high priest and others, "It is as you said. Nevertheless, I say to you, hereafter you will see the Son of Man sitting at the right hand of the Power, and coming on the clouds of heaven" (Matthew 26:64). This statement provoked outrage from the high priest, who saw it as blasphemous and grounds for Jesus' execution. The parallel passage in Mark 14:62 says, "I am. And you will see the Son of Man sitting at the right hand of the Power, and coming with the clouds of heaven."

The imagery of returning with clouds aligns with the account of Jesus' ascension in the book of Acts. In Acts 1:11, two angels told those at the ascension, "Men of Galilee, why do you stand gazing up into heaven? This same Jesus, who was taken up from you into heaven, will so come in like manner as you saw Him go into heaven." Jesus will clearly return on clouds at his second coming, fulfilling predictions by the Old Testament prophets and his own predictions.

73. WHERE WILL JESUS RETURN?

When Jesus returns at the second coming, where will he be located?

The Bible gives clear information about the actual site where we can expect Jesus to arrive. The Mount of Olives is the specific site of Jesus' second coming. Zechariah 14:4 predicts, "In that day His feet will stand on the Mount of Olives, which faces Jerusalem on the east. And the Mount of Olives shall be split in two, from east to west, making a very large valley; half of the mountain shall move toward the north and half of it toward the south."

This location is important due to other key events that have taken place at the Mount of Olives. Jesus addressed questions about the end of the age with his disciples from this same location in Matthew 24:3: "Now as He sat on the Mount of Olives, the disciples came to Him privately, saying, 'Tell us, when will these things be? And what will be the sign of Your coming, and of the end of the age?'"

Jesus also traveled to the Mount of Olives ahead of his entry into Jerusalem on the day known as Palm Sunday. He sent two of his followers from this location to find the young donkey he would ride into the city: "It came to pass, when He drew near to Bethphage and Bethany, at the mountain called Olivet, that He sent two of His disciples, saying, 'Go into the village opposite you, where as you enter you will find a colt tied, on which no one has ever sat. Loose it and bring it here'" (Luke 19:29–30).

During the week before Jesus' crucifixion, the Mount of Olives was the location where he stayed with his disciples: "In the daytime He was teaching in the temple, but at night He went out and stayed on the mountain called Olivet" (Luke 21:37).

The Mount of Olives is known as the location where Jesus ascended to heaven forty days after his resurrection. Acts 1:12 says they left the ascension from this significant point: "Then they returned to Jerusalem from the mount called Olivet, which is near Jerusalem, a Sabbath day's journey."

The Mount of Olives is significant for its role during the ministry of Jesus, his ascension, and his second coming. One day Christ will return to this location to fulfill the very prophecies he made about himself there on the land where he last laid his head to rest during his earthly life.

74. What Is the Relationship between Ezekiel's Temple and the Millennial Kingdom?

The prophet Ezekiel describes a future Jewish temple in Ezekiel 40–48 that does not fit the temple that existed during the earthly life of Jesus. How do Ezekiel's predictions relate to the future temple predicted in the millennial kingdom in Revelation 20?

Ezekiel provides a vision of a new, magnificent temple that will exist in the future. This vision includes the return of God's glory (chapter 43), the practice of animal sacrifices (chapters 44–46), and the restoration of the land to the people (chapters 47–48). The people's hearts will be renewed (36:26–27), and even gentiles will have a place in this restored kingdom (47:22). The land will be governed by a Davidic ruler (44:3).

In his vision, Ezekiel was brought to a location in Israel where he saw a mountain and a city. He met an angelic being he described as "a man whose appearance was like the appearance of bronze. He had a line of flax and a measuring rod in his hand, and he stood in the gateway" (40:3). The man instructed Ezekiel to carefully observe everything he saw and heard, including the detailed measurements of the temple area.

Many who expect a literal fulfillment anticipate that the temple will be built during the millennium, the future thousand-year reign of Christ that will follow his second coming. During this period, glorified saints will interact with people who still need to choose faith in Christ, which many will not. In this view, the sacrificial system described by Ezekiel is not for atonement since Christ's sacrifice has already achieved that. Instead, these sacrifices might serve as memorials or rites of ceremonial purification.

Some take Ezekiel's temple figuratively, believing Ezekiel's vision symbolizes the restoration of God's perfect relationship with his people. This vision employs imagery familiar to Ezekiel and his audience, including a grand temple with regular sacrifices and the visible presence of God's glory.

Later prophetic visions reveal that the Messiah would fulfill these promises by replacing the temple, sacrifices, and land with the presence of the Holy Spirit. Those who hold this view interpret Ezekiel's temple as a partial fulfillment in the church age in anticipation of a complete realization in the future.

While either view is possible and is difficult to determine for certain, Ezekiel's vision of a future temple appears to closely align with the predictions of Revelation 20:1–6. Christ will one day reign with his people from his throne in Jerusalem, and Ezekiel's temple will be the place of worship. If so, this fulfillment will reveal God's amazing ability to predict future events in a spectacular manner, giving Ezekiel insight into this future time thousands of years in advance.

75. IS THE MILLENNIAL KINGDOM A LITERAL THOUSAND-YEAR PERIOD OR IS IT SYMBOLIC?

Revelation 20:1–7 depicts a future period known as "the millennial kingdom," during which Scripture says Jesus will reign on earth for a thousand years. This raises the question: Should we interpret this as a literal thousand-year reign?

A straightforward reading of Revelation 20 emphasizes the term "one thousand years," which appears six times within these seven verses. This repeated usage suggests that John intended this period to be understood literally rather than figuratively.

Some argue that the number might be symbolic, referencing 2 Peter 3:8, which states, "Beloved, do not forget this one thing, that with the Lord one day is as a thousand years, and a thousand years as one day." However, the context of this verse focuses on the patience of God in delaying Christ's return to allow more time for repentance and faith rather than offering a direct explanation of the millennial reign.

Moreover, the literal interpretation of the thousand-year period is significant because it aligns with other biblical prophecies regarding the Messiah's future rule. For instance, Luke 1:31–32 foretells that Jesus will receive "the throne of His father David," implying a future reign in Jerusalem. This promise underscores the expectation that Jesus will fulfill the role of king in a tangible, earthly kingdom.

The covenants made by God also support the notion of a literal reign. The Abrahamic covenant includes a promise to Abraham that his descendants would inherit the land and rule over it (Genesis 12:1–3).

God also promised David that his lineage would establish a kingdom forever, as stated in 2 Samuel 7:12–13: "I will set up your seed after you, who will come from your body, and I will establish his kingdom. He shall build a house for My name, and I will establish the throne of his kingdom forever." These covenants imply a real, lasting rule that Jesus will establish, which aligns with the concept of a literal thousand-year reign.

Zechariah 8:3 adds further context by declaring that the Lord will return to Jerusalem and dwell there, making it the "City of Truth" and the "Mountain of the Lord of hosts." Some interpret this as a past fulfillment, but the passage is often seen as pointing to a future event when Jesus will reign from Jerusalem, reflecting the establishment of his millennial kingdom.

Considering alternative interpretations, a figurative or allegorical approach to the "thousand years" would require reconciling the term with the specifics of biblical prophecy. If not taken literally, the symbolic interpretation would need to adequately address the numerous references to this period and their implications for the Messiah's reign. The literal interpretation best fits the context of prophecies and promises regarding Christ's earthly kingdom.

At the conclusion of the millennial kingdom, Revelation 20:7–15 describes, will be a final rebellion led by Satan, which Jesus will swiftly defeat. This will be followed by the final judgment and the creation of a new heaven and a new earth, including a New Jerusalem where God's people will dwell eternally (Revelation 21–22). This ultimate fulfillment of God's promises highlights the significance of the millennial reign as a precursor to the eternal state.

76. What Is the Purpose of the Millennial Kingdom?

The millennial kingdom refers to the thousand-year reign following the tribulation and before the final judgment. But what is the purpose of this earthly reign that will take place before the new heavens and earth?

During this period, Jesus will rule as king over Israel and all the nations (Isaiah 2:4). This era will be marked by global peace (Isaiah 11:6–9; 32:18), the binding of Satan (Revelation 20:1–3), and the worship of God (Isaiah 2:2–3). The main purpose of this reign will be to fulfill God's covenants.

The Abrahamic covenant, which promised Abraham land, numerous descendants, and a blessing to many nations, has been partially fulfilled. Abraham did enter the promised land and become the leader of nations through his descendants.

But Israel has never fully possessed the boundaries described in Genesis 15:18–20 and Numbers 34:1–12. Even Solomon's reign, which included the land from the border of Egypt to the Euphrates, did not cover the entire area outlined in these Scripture verses. The covenant specified that the land would be an everlasting possession for Abraham and his descendants (Genesis 13:15; 17:8; Ezekiel 16:60). While modern Israel includes some of this land, the nation does not yet occupy the full extent of the land described by God.

In addition, God promised in the Davidic covenant that David's lineage would endure forever and that his descendant would reign on Israel's throne perpetually: "Your house and your kingdom shall be established forever before you. Your throne shall be established forever" (2 Samuel 7:16). The coming of Jesus fulfills this covenant, evident in the genealogies provided in Matthew 1:1–17 and Luke 3:23–38.

The expectation among Jews when Jesus entered Jerusalem was that he would be a political and military leader who would restore Israel's sovereignty. However, his mission was to establish the new covenant rather than fulfill the Davidic covenant at that time. The millennium will mark the beginning of Jesus' reign over both Israel and the earth.

Third, the new covenant, foretold in Jeremiah 31:31–34, involves Jesus' death and resurrection, which were intended to reconcile humanity to God. Although this covenant has been inaugurated, we still await its complete fulfillment. Jeremiah 31:33 promises that God's law will be inscribed on the hearts of his people, while Ezekiel 36:28 specifies that the Israelites will dwell in their land and be God's people.

In addition to these covenants, other promises will also be fulfilled during the millennial kingdom. Jesus will defeat his enemies, and his followers will worship him freely (Psalm 110). The nations will then experience peace under Jesus' rule: "To Him was given dominion and glory and a kingdom, that all peoples, nations, and languages should serve Him. His dominion is an everlasting dominion, which shall not pass away, and His kingdom the one which shall not be destroyed" (Daniel 7:14). The millennial kingdom's primary purpose is to fulfill these prophecies. God's covenants include aspects that remain unfulfilled today but will be realized during this important future time.

77. Who Will Live in the Millennial Kingdom?

Revelation 20 outlines a millennial kingdom where Jesus will live with his people for one thousand years. Who will be with the Lord during this future time?

First, believers who are raptured to be with Christ will be with Jesus during the millennial kingdom. The words of 1 Thessalonians 4:17 promise "we shall always be with the Lord."

Revelation 20:4 describes a second group that will be present in the millennial kingdom:

> I saw thrones, and they sat on them, and judgment was committed to them. Then I saw the souls of those who had been beheaded for their witness to Jesus and for the word of God, who had not worshiped the beast or his image, and had not received his mark on their foreheads or on their hands. And they lived and reigned with Christ for a thousand years.

Third, faithful believers from before Christ's death and resurrection will dwell in this future millennial kingdom. These will include God's followers from the past, such as Abraham, Moses, Elijah, and many others who believed in the Lord before the coming of Jesus the Messiah.

One final group of individuals will also live in this kingdom. They will include people who become believers during the seven-year tribulation and enter the millennial kingdom alive. These new believers will experience extended lifespans, marriage, and childbearing (Isaiah 65:20–25). Referring to long lifespans during this time, verse 20 predicts, "No more shall an infant from there live but a few days, nor an old man who has not fulfilled his days; for the child shall die one hundred years old, but the sinner being one hundred years old shall be accursed."

During the millennial kingdom, all these individuals will live under Christ's reign with Satan bound, leading to a time of relative peace. While the full effects of sin will not be eradicated until the creation of the new heavens and new earth (Revelation 21–22), many of its consequences will be removed, as people will live longer, peace will prevail, and Satan will be restrained.

Many details of life during the millennium remain unclear. It is clear, however, that those who believe in the Lord now will be with him during this time. This period will also fulfill God's remaining prophecies and promises to his people. As believers, we can look forward to this unique future time with the Lord when he will reign and we will live in his presence.

78. Will There Be Animal Sacrifice During the Millennial Kingdom?

Some people wonder about the mention of sacrifices in the millennial kingdom since this practice is mentioned in the vision of Ezekiel's future temple. Will there really be sacrifices during this future time?

It may seem unusual, but the Bible does indicate that animal sacrifices will be practiced during the millennial kingdom. Ezekiel chapters 43 through 46 provide detailed prophecies about these practices, focusing on the Jewish temple during this period. The line of Zadok is mentioned as offering sacrifices

(44:15), including sacrifices of rams, lambs, and bulls outlined in Ezekiel 45 and 46.

Isaiah also references sacrifices in the future millennial kingdom, saying, "Even them I will bring to My holy mountain, and make them joyful in My house of prayer. Their burnt offerings and their sacrifices will be accepted on My altar; for My house shall be called a house of prayer for all nations" (Isaiah 56:7).

Similarly, Zechariah 14:16 notes that all survivors from the nations that opposed Jerusalem will annually visit to worship the King and celebrate the Feast of Booths, which would include sacrifices: "It shall come to pass that everyone who is left of all the nations which came against Jerusalem shall go up from year to year to worship the King, the Lord of hosts, and to keep the Feast of Tabernacles."

Jeremiah 33:17–18 adds that the Levitical priests will always be present to offer burnt offerings, grain offerings, and sacrifices during this time: "Thus says the Lord: 'David shall never lack a man to sit on the throne of the house of Israel; nor shall the priests, the Levites, lack a man to offer burnt offerings before Me, to kindle grain offerings, and to sacrifice continually.'"

Some argue against the continuation of animal sacrifices in the millennial kingdom, citing that the sacrifice of Christ on the cross should have rendered such practices unnecessary. Hebrews 10:11–12 explains that while priests repeatedly offered sacrifices that could not take away sins, Christ's sacrifice ended the need for these ongoing offerings.

The Bible does not provide a full explanation, but the continuation of sacrifices during the millennial kingdom will serve as a fulfillment of Old Testament prophecies. If these sacrifices were not to occur, it would be a failure to fulfill God's promises, yet God is always faithful to keep his word.

In the Old Testament, animal sacrifices did not remove sin but were acts of obedience and repentance. Similarly, during the millennial kingdom, these future sacrifices will not atone for sin but will serve as a memorial to God. Under Christ's reign, these offerings will gain new significance as Jesus rules as Messiah and King.

79. What Will Happen to Satan during and after the Millennial Kingdom?

At the end of the tribulation, Jesus will return and defeat Satan before reigning in his millennial kingdom. What will happen to Satan during this time?

Revelation 20:1–3 describes the first part of this question:

> Then I saw an angel coming down from heaven, having the key to the bottomless pit and a great chain in his hand. He laid hold of the dragon, that serpent of old, who is the Devil and Satan, and bound him for a thousand years; and he cast him into the bottomless pit, and shut him up, and set a seal on him, so that he should deceive the nations no more till the thousand years were finished. But after these things he must be released for a little while.

Satan will be bound and cast into the bottomless pit for one thousand years. This marks the entire period of the millennial kingdom. He will not be able to operate on earth during this time.

Revelation 20:7–8 describes a significant event at the end of the millennial kingdom, where Satan will be released from his imprisonment and gather the nations, including Gog and Magog, for a final battle against God and his people: "Now when the thousand years have expired, Satan will be released from his prison and will go out to deceive the nations which are in the four corners of the earth, Gog and Magog, to gather them together to battle, whose number is as the sand of the sea."

Why would God allow Satan to be released for yet another rebellion against him? Revelation 21–22 depicts the creation of a new heaven and earth free from sin and the curse. Before this transformation occurs, God addresses the final rebellion by removing Satan, the beast, the false prophet, and their followers.

Revelation 20:9–10 states that fire will descend from heaven, consuming these enemies, and Satan will be cast into the lake of fire, where he will be tormented eternally: "They went up on the breadth of the earth and surrounded the camp of the saints and the beloved city. And fire came down from God out of heaven and devoured them. The devil, who deceived them, was cast into the lake of fire and brimstone where the beast and the false prophet are. And they will be tormented day and night forever and ever."

During this period, the unbelievers who will participate in this final battle are likely those who have survived the tribulation and entered the millennium in their mortal state. These individuals will have children, some of whom may reject faith in God and align with Satan. Revelation 20:8 describes these unbelievers as numerous, like "the sand of the sea," suggesting a vast number of people who will ultimately side with Satan.

Although Scripture does not fully detail the specific reasons why God will allow this final battle, the primary purpose is evident: it signifies the ultimate eradication of evil and sin. With Satan and sin removed, God's people will live with him forever in a perfect, sinless new creation.

80. What Will Occur at the Final Judgment?

Revelation 20 records a final judgment before God creates a new heavens and earth. What will happen during this time?

Revelation 20:11–15 describes the great white throne judgment, the final assessment before the lost are cast into the lake of fire. This judgment occurs after the millennial kingdom and after Satan, along with the beast and the false prophet, have been thrown into the lake of fire (vv. 7–10).

During this judgment, the deeds of everyone, whether good or evil, are reviewed: "I saw the dead, small and great, standing before God, and books were opened. And another book was opened, which is the Book of Life. And the dead were judged according to their works, by the things which were written in the books" (v. 12).

God's comprehensive knowledge encompasses every action, word, and thought, and he will provide rewards or punishment based on this record. The Book of Life will also be opened (v. 12), which will determine whether an individual will receive eternal life or face eternal punishment. Christians, whose names are written in this book "from the foundation of the world" (17:8), are forgiven through Christ and are judged differently. The judgment will reveal that those not found in the Book of Life will be cast into the lake of fire (20:15).

The concept of a final judgment for all people, both believers and nonbelievers, is supported by multiple Scripture passages. While the great white throne judgment is depicted as the ultimate judgment, interpretations vary among Christians regarding its relationship to other biblical judgments.

Some Christians believe that three distinct judgments are described in the Bible. The first is the judgment of the sheep and the goats (the judgment of the nations), occurring after the tribulation but before the millennium, which determines who will enter the millennial kingdom (Matthew 25:31–36).

The second is the judgment of believers' works, known as the "judgment seat of Christ" (2 Corinthians 5:10), where Christians receive rewards based on their service to God.

The third is the great white throne judgment at the end of the millennium focusing on the judgment of unbelievers and their ultimate punishment.

Other Christians interpret these judgments as describing different aspects of the same final event. According to this view, the great white throne judgment encompasses the assessment of both believers and unbelievers. Believers' deeds are evaluated to determine their rewards, while unbelievers are judged for the severity of their punishment. Supporters of this view see Matthew 25:31–46 as another perspective on the great white throne judgment, aligning the results with those described in Revelation 20:11–15, where believers are granted eternal life and unbelievers face eternal punishment.

Regardless of the interpretation, several key points remain consistent. Jesus Christ will be the judge of all, and unbelievers will face judgment based on their deeds, resulting in punishment. The Bible emphasizes that unbelievers are storing up wrath for themselves (Romans 2:5) and will be repaid according to their actions (v. 6). Believers, covered by Christ's righteousness and whose names are in the Book of Life, will be rewarded according to their deeds, not punished.

As Romans 14:12 indicates, everyone will give an account to God before the judgment seat of Christ: "Each of us shall give account of himself to God."

SECTION 9

THE NEW HEAVENS AND NEW EARTH

81. What Are the New Heavens and New Earth in Revelation?

Revelation 21:1 mentions a new heavens and new earth. These future creations appear designed to replace the current heavens and earth, but what will they be like?

The text of Revelation 21:1–4 describes these new realities in this way:

> I saw a new heaven and a new earth, for the first heaven and the first earth had passed away. Also there was no more sea. Then I, John, saw the holy city, New Jerusalem, coming down out of heaven from God, prepared as a bride adorned for her husband. And I heard a loud voice from heaven saying, "Behold, the tabernacle of God is with men, and He will dwell with them, and they shall be His people. God Himself will be with them and be their God. And God will wipe away every tear from their eyes; there shall be no more

> death, nor sorrow, nor crying. There shall be no more pain, for the former things have passed away."

Several observations can be made based on these verses. First, the current heavens and earth will pass away. Some believe the heavens and earth will be remade, but it is more likely we will live in a completely new reality.

Second, the new earth will include a New Jerusalem. This heavenly city will be the focal point of God's future creation, where God will dwell with his people and believers will worship him forever: "He carried me away in the Spirit to a great and high mountain, and showed me the great city, the holy Jerusalem, descending out of heaven from God, having the glory of God" (21:10–11). The city will be radiant, extending over fourteen hundred miles in all directions (v. 16).

Third, the new heavens and earth are defined by the many ways they contrast with our current world. There will be no tears, death, sorrow, crying, or pain. The negative emotions and suffering we experience in our lives are temporary for those who believe. In eternity, there will be "no more pain."

Revelation 22:15 notes that this situation will remain permanent. Those who rejected Christ will not be later allowed into the new heavens and new earth. Instead, they will be outside: "Outside are dogs and sorcerers and sexually immoral and murderers and idolaters, and whoever loves and practices a lie."

Revelation 22:3 reveals that there will be no more curse in heaven. Sin will be removed in the new heavens and earth. This joyous prediction led the apostle John to end Revelation with this plea: "Even so, come, Lord Jesus!" (v. 20).

This is a glorious future to look forward to today. Your pain may weaken your experience today, but it won't weaken eternity. Our aches, pains, struggles, and temptations will be replaced with the presence of the Lord in a new world filled with joy and delight as we experience fellowship with believers from throughout history and join in worshiping our King.

82. WHAT WILL WE LOOK LIKE IN HEAVEN?

Many people wonder what we will look like in heaven. Will we be young and full of life, or will we be the same age as when we die? What about infants or young children who pass away? Will they remain in a child's body?

The Bible does not answer every detail we would like about this question, but it does give us some information about what to anticipate. In 1 Corinthians 15:42–55, the apostle Paul discusses the "incorruptible" bodies we will have in heaven. Through Paul, we learn that these future heavenly bodies will be glorious, powerful, and spiritual. We will also be changed from our current body to a heavenly body, though Paul appears to shift focus to the rapture in verse 51. Our body will be eternal, strong, and spiritual in heaven.

In some ways, the post-resurrection body of Jesus could also offer some insights into what to expect. He was clearly recognizable, including his scars. However, his new body was healthy and even somehow able to pass through locked doors (John 21:19, 26).

What is not clearly noted is what age we will appear in heaven. Since heaven is eternal, we won't age. Instead, we'll likely have a new body that eternally appears at its optimal, perfect stage of development. Those in wheelchairs or with walkers won't need them while young children who passed away will likely be in their fully matured bodies in eternity, though the Bible does not specifically speak to this aspect regarding children.

Another example can be found in the account of the transfiguration of Jesus. In Matthew 17:1–8, Moses and Elijah appeared with Jesus. They were clearly recognizable in their heavenly bodies.

In 1 John 3:2 we are told, "Beloved, now we are children of God; and it has not yet been revealed what we shall be, but we know that when He is revealed, we shall be like Him, for we shall see Him as He is." As believers, we can take comfort that we will be like the Lord in heaven, meaning we will have an eternal body that does not wear out and can completely enjoy every moment with the Lord and his people.

Revelation 22 also explains that we will live in a world without the curse in the new heavens and new earth. We will be able to eat and drink even though we will not need to eat or drink to survive. Verse 14 indicates there will also be people wearing robes in heaven. It appears that we'll be wearing clothing perfectly designed for our time in heaven. There will no longer be sickness or sin or death, but instead, a perfect future where any unknown details will be divinely answered by the constant and direct presence of our Lord.

83. What Will the New Heavens and Earth Be Like?

The final two chapters of the Bible, Revelation 21–22, describe a new heaven and earth the Lord will create following the millennial kingdom and his final judgment. What can we know about this future eternal home of all believers?

Several details are described in these two key chapters about eternity. First, there will be no more sea (21:1).

Second, a new holy city called the "New Jerusalem" will come down from the sky: "Then I, John, saw the holy city, New Jerusalem, coming down out of heaven from God, prepared as a bride adorned for her husband" (v. 2).

Third, God will be with his people (v. 3): "Behold, the tabernacle of God is with men, and He will dwell with them, and they shall be His people. God Himself will be with them and be their God."

Fourth, pain and suffering will end: "God will wipe away every tear from their eyes; there shall be no more death, nor sorrow, nor crying. There shall be no more pain, for the former things have passed away" (v. 4).

Fifth, we will drink from the fountain of the water of life: "I will give of the fountain of the water of life freely to him who thirsts" (v. 6).

Sixth, as seen in Revelation 22:1–2, the new heavens will be beautiful: "He showed me a pure river of water of life, clear as crystal, proceeding from the throne of God and of the Lamb. In the middle of its street, and on either side of the river, was the tree of life, which bore twelve fruits, each tree yielding its fruit every month. The leaves of the tree were for the healing of the nations."

Seventh, sin will be removed: "There shall be no more curse, but the throne of God and of the Lamb shall be in it, and His servants shall serve Him" (v. 3).

All believers will see God's face and live forever in his presence: "They shall see His face, and His name shall be on their foreheads. There shall be no night there: They need no lamp nor light of the sun, for the Lord God gives them light. And they shall reign forever and ever" (vv. 4–5).

We are not told the size of the new heavens and earth, as they will be beyond comprehension. The scale of the New Jerusalem alone will far surpass anything in our current reality, described as about fourteen thousand miles in each direction (21:15–17). These details Scripture does reveal offer a small look into the astounding eternal home where all believers will dwell with one another and the Lord for all eternity.

84. What is the New Jerusalem?

The New Jerusalem is depicted in the Bible as a heavenly city that will exist upon the new earth at the end of time, with a detailed description provided in Revelation 21:9–27. What does the Bible say about this new heavenly city?

First, its origin is described as celestial: "He carried me away in the Spirit to a great and high mountain, and showed me the great city, the holy Jerusalem, descending out of heaven from God, having the glory of God" (vv. 10–11). In addition, its appearance is marked by divine splendor: "Her light was like a most precious stone, like a jasper stone, clear as crystal" (v. 11).

The city's structure is outlined with specific majestic features:

> Also she had a great and high wall with twelve gates, and twelve angels at the gates, and names written on them, which are the names of the twelve tribes of the children of Israel: three gates on the east, three gates on the north, three gates on the south, and three gates on the west.
>
> Now the wall of the city had twelve foundations, and on them were the names of the twelve apostles of the Lamb. (vv. 12–14)

The city's size is also described in detail:

> He who talked with me had a gold reed to measure the city, its gates, and its wall. The city is laid out as a square; its length is as great as its breadth. And he measured the city with the reed: twelve thousand furlongs. Its length, breadth, and height are equal. Then he measured its wall: one hundred and forty-four cubits, according to the measure of a man, that is, of an angel. (vv. 15–17)

This equates to about fourteen thousand miles in each direction by modern standards, with most interpreting the shape as a cube, though some suggest a pyramid form.

The city's construction materials are described in terms of grandeur:

> The construction of its wall was of jasper; and the city was pure gold, like clear glass. The foundations of the wall of the city were adorned with all kinds of precious stones: the first foundation was jasper, the second

> sapphire, the third chalcedony, the fourth emerald, the fifth sardonyx, the sixth sardius, the seventh chrysolite, the eighth beryl, the ninth topaz, the tenth chrysoprase, the eleventh jacinth, and the twelfth amethyst. The twelve gates were twelve pearls: each individual gate was of one pearl. And the street of the city was pure gold, like transparent glass. (vv. 18–21)

The descriptions highlight a level of beauty far beyond any earthly city.

The city's illumination is provided by the Lord:

> I saw no temple in it, for the Lord God Almighty and the Lamb are its temple. The city had no need of the sun or of the moon to shine in it, for the glory of God illuminated it. The Lamb is its light. And the nations of those who are saved shall walk in its light, and the kings of the earth bring their glory and honor into it. Its gates shall not be shut at all by day (there shall be no night there). (vv. 22–25)

In this divine city, God and the Lamb will be both temple and source of light.

The inhabitants are described as follows: "They shall bring the glory and the honor of the nations into it. But there shall by no means enter it anything that defiles, or causes an abomination or a lie, but only those who are written in the Lamb's Book of Life" (vv. 26–27). Only those whose names are recorded in the Lamb's Book of Life will reside there, ensuring the city remains pure and filled with the glory of God.

85. WILL WE RECOGNIZE OUR FAMILY MEMBERS AND FRIENDS IN HEAVEN?

Some have asked us whether we will recognize our family members and friends in heaven. If we have new bodies, how will we know those around us?

For believers, one of the greatest blessings of heaven will be the presence of their loved ones—family and friends who have preceded them in faith. We will see, recognize, and spend time with these cherished individuals for all eternity in heaven. While the ultimate joy will come from our relationship with our Lord and Savior, the experience will be shared with fellow believers, including our family members and other loved ones.

Although the Bible offers limited details about recognizing others in the afterlife, there are some references. For instance, David expressed confidence that he would recognize his deceased infant son in heaven, as he said, "I shall go to him, but he shall not return to me" (2 Samuel 12:23). This statement suggests that David expected to see his son as an individual, rather than as just another soul.

Similarly, in the parable of the rich man and Lazarus (Luke 16:19–31), the figures of Abraham, Lazarus, and the rich man were identifiable after death. The rich man was able to recognize Lazarus at Abraham's side despite the great chasm between them. This narrative does not confirm that we will see those in hell, but it may suggest that those in hell might be able to see those in heaven, potentially heightening their suffering. The joy of heaven might be preserved by shielding the righteous from seeing those in hell, ensuring their joy remains undisturbed (Psalm 16:11).

At the transfiguration of Jesus in Matthew 17 and Mark 9, the three disciples Peter, James, and John recognized Moses and Elijah when they appeared with Jesus. Despite new bodies, Moses and Elijah could still be identified, offering hope that we will recognize our loved ones in heaven as well.

Following his resurrection, many recognized Jesus, including his disciples (John 20:16, 20; 21:12). Since believers are promised glorified bodies similar to Jesus' (1 John 3:2; 1 Corinthians 15:49, 53), it is reasonable to expect that we will recognize each other in heaven.

Another concept relevant to this question is the Bible's promise that we will know more in heaven, not less. Paul wrote in 1 Corinthians 13:12: "Now I know in part, but then I shall know just as I also am known."

Even if we find it difficult to imagine heaven without those who have died without Christ, the joy of heaven will remain complete. The ultimate joy will come from being in the presence of God, free from the constraints of sin. Worshiping our Lord and Savior will provide eternal bliss, and the opportunity to know and be known by him and fellow believers will be a source of immense joy.

86. How Can Heaven Be Perfect if Some of Our Loved Ones Are Not There?

Concerns about some of our loved ones not being in heaven are among the most difficult questions we face. This question often arises during funerals, as individuals reflect on the afterlife. How can heaven be perfect when a person we dearly love is not there with us?

First, we can take comfort that the Bible assures us God will eliminate all sorrow and pain from the heavenly experience. Revelation 21:4 promises, "God will wipe away every tear from their eyes; there shall be no more death, nor sorrow, nor crying. There shall be no more pain, for the former things have passed away." While the Bible does not detail exactly how this will occur, it assures us that it will.

This verse also says the old order of things will end. This suggests that any grief related to loved ones not present in heaven may be transformed or removed. The following verse adds, "Then He who sat on the throne said, 'Behold, I make all things new'" (v. 5). God might erase these memories or alter our perceptions to align with his perfect understanding. Although specifics are not provided, it is clear that our existence in heaven will be free from sadness.

Another insight may be found in the account of Lazarus and the rich man in Luke 16:19–31. The rich man was in torment in the afterlife, asking Abraham to send help to his unbelieving family to warn them about future judgment. Lazarus, who was with Abraham in the Lord's presence, did not express concerns about those who were not with him. He was described as being carried by the angels to Abraham's side.

Verse 25 said Lazarus was "comforted." Details are not given, but it is clear that Lazarus was not sad over any of his loved ones who were not in heaven with him. Instead, the emphasis was on the good things he experienced in the afterlife that stood in contrast with the struggles he faced during his earthly life.

In 1 Corinthians 2:9, the apostle Paul also reminds us that "eye has not seen, nor ear heard, nor have entered into the heart of man the things which God has prepared for those who love Him." There is much we do not understand about heaven, but we do know God has prepared a home for those who believe in him. There, we will enjoy eternity. We will not be saddened over those who are not there but will rejoice in the Lord's presence and with his people forever.

Even if we do not have all the answers that we would like concerning this issue, we can trust in the promise of Psalm 18:30: "As for God, His way is perfect." When we are united with Christ, what seems incomprehensible now will become clear in the light of eternity. We will worship him who makes all things perfect.

87. WILL WE EAT IN HEAVEN?

Many people wonder if we will eat food in heaven. This curiosity stems from the belief that the enjoyable aspects of earthly life, such as relationships and experiences, might be present in heaven as well.

For example, Jesus mentioned eating and drinking in the kingdom when he celebrated the Passover with his disciples shortly before his crucifixion. He said, "Assuredly, I say to you, I will no longer drink of the fruit of the vine until that day when I drink it new in the kingdom of God" (Mark 14:25).

This suggests that in the millennial kingdom, which is a period following Christ's return and during which his followers will have their resurrection bodies, eating and drinking will occur. However, the specifics about eating in the new heavens and earth may be different.

In John's vision of the New Jerusalem, he describes "a pure river of water of life, clear as crystal, proceeding from the throne of God and of the Lamb. In the middle of its street, and on either side of the river, was the tree of life, which bore twelve fruits, each tree yielding its fruit every month" (Revelation 22:1–2). We are promised that food and water will exist in heaven, though these verses do not specifically say we will eat or drink during this time.

Some suggest that we will eat and drink in heaven because Adam and Eve ate in the garden of Eden before sin entered humanity. While this is possible, there will be many differences between the world in which Adam and Eve lived and the future eternity where God's people will dwell.

Others note that Jesus ate after his resurrection. He ate broiled fish in Luke 24:42–43 and appears to have eaten fish with some of his followers in John 21. Again, this points to the possibility of believers eating in heaven, but it does not prove this will be the case.

Luke 13:29 reveals Jesus telling a parable, stating that people will take their places at the feast in the kingdom of God. This future feast may refer to a time of eating in the afterlife, hinting again at food as part of our eternal existence. If we do eat, it won't be out of necessity. Instead, eating and drinking will serve as part of the joy of heaven as we celebrate the presence of God with his people.

Ultimately, the answer to whether we will eat in heaven is not fully revealed. As believers, we understand only in part (1 Corinthians 13:9). The full experience of being in the presence of our Savior, who is described as "the bread of life" (John 6:35), transcends our current understanding.

88. Will We See Our Pets in Heaven?

Many of us cherish our pets, finding that their presence enriches our lives. Whether it's the joyful wag of a dog's tail when we come home, the comforting purr of a cat nestled on our lap on a chilly evening, or the awe-inspiring sight of a horse galloping across a field, animals bring a unique and profound joy. Will we one day be reunited with our pets in heaven?

It's only natural to wish our pets might be with us in heaven. The Bible affirms that animals were created by God and are an integral part of his creation (Genesis 1:25). However, the Bible does not specifically address whether animals will be present in heaven. Unlike humans, who have the opportunity to choose eternal life through Jesus Christ, animals cannot make such a choice. This implies that animals may not have the same access to heaven as humans do.

In Ecclesiastes 3:21, Solomon asks, "Who knows if the human spirit rises upward and if the spirit of the animal goes down into the earth?" (NIV). This question leaves the answer open-ended regarding whether animals that die on earth will be in heaven. Solomon, known as the world's wisest man during his time, was apparently uncertain about the eternal destiny of animal life.

The Bible does suggest that animals will be present on the new earth (Genesis 9:15–17; Ecclesiastes 3:18–21; Isaiah 11:6–9; Luke 3:6; Romans 8:19–21; Revelation 5:13). Animals will also exist during the millennial kingdom (Isaiah 11:6; 65:25).

However, whether these will include the exact animals or pets we knew on earth is not specified.

When it comes to talking about the loss of someone's pet, it is important to be sensitive. Proverbs 12:10 teaches that a righteous person cares about his or her animals. We can be caring in the way we talk about the loss of a pet, realizing that for many people this animal also connects with many memories and relationships in life.

In the end, the Bible does not give us all the details we may wish on this topic. The best we can say about whether our pets will be in heaven is *maybe*. What is certain is that our joy in heaven will be complete, regardless of whether our pets are present.

The happiness we experience will come from being in the direct presence of God and enjoying a state of perfect, sinless fellowship with him. There will be no sorrow regardless of whether our earthly pets join us in heaven (Revelation 21:4).

89. IS THERE A LITERAL HELL, AND WHAT WILL HAPPEN TO PEOPLE IN HELL DURING THE NEW HEAVENS AND EARTH?

The concept of heaven is appealing to many, but the idea of hell is often met with discomfort. These negative feelings about hell have led many to reject that a literal hell exists. Is hell a real place? If so, what will happen there?

The Bible's descriptions of hell are concerning. Scripture portrays hell as a realm of "everlasting fire" (Matthew 25:41), "unquenchable fire" (3:12), and a place of "shame and everlasting contempt" (Daniel 12:2). It is described as a place where "the fire is not quenched" (Mark 9:44–49), there is "everlasting destruction" (2 Thessalonians 1:9), and "the smoke of their torment ascends forever and ever" (Revelation 14:10–11).

In Luke 16:24–26, Jesus explained hell as a place of anguish and fire:

> Then he cried and said, "Father Abraham, have mercy on me, and send Lazarus that he may dip the tip of his finger in water and cool my tongue; for I am tormented in this flame." But Abraham said, "Son, remember that in your lifetime you received your good things, and likewise Lazarus evil things; but now he is comforted and you are tormented. And besides all this, between us and you there is a great gulf fixed, so that those who want to pass from here to you cannot, nor can those from there pass to us."

These words reveal hell's torment, flames, and the inability to leave.

Revelation 20:10 depicts the future home of unbelievers in the most dreadful manner: "The devil, who deceived them, was cast into the lake of fire and brimstone where the beast and the false prophet are. And they will be tormented day and night forever and ever." Jesus affirmed that the punishment in hell is as enduring as the joy of heaven (Matthew 25:46).

Revelation 21:8 clearly shows that those in the lake of fire will remain outside of God's presence forever: "The cowardly, unbelieving, abominable, murderers, sexually immoral, sorcerers, idolaters, and all liars shall have their part in the lake which burns with fire and brimstone, which is the second death."

Eternity is a certainty for everyone; the issue is the location. The righteous, whose sins are redeemed through Christ's sacrifice, will experience eternal joy in heaven. In contrast, the wicked will endure God's wrath and the eternal consequences of their actions in hell, recognizing the justice of their punishment.

Hell is undeniably a real and horrifying place of perpetual torment. The only escape from this grim reality is through the cross, where forgiveness of sins is offered. Without this, people will face infinite suffering in hell.

90. ARE SATAN AND DEMONS REAL? IF SO, WHAT ARE THEIR ROLES IN TODAY'S WORLD?

The Bible identifies Satan as a real and formidable adversary (Genesis 3:15). He is referred to as the "accuser" of believers (Revelation 12:10), and the term "Satan" itself translates to "adversary."

Originally known as Lucifer, Satan fell from grace due to his pride and desire for divine glory, leading to his rebellion against God and expulsion from heaven along with a third of the angels who followed him (Isaiah 14:12–17; Ezekiel 28:11–17). Since his fall, Satan has been committed to opposing God, aiming to deceive and lead people into rebellion. Paul describes him as "the god of this world" (2 Corinthians 4:4 KJV) and "the prince of the power of the air" (Ephesians 2:2).

Deception is Satan's primary weapon. This was evident when he tempted Adam and Eve in the garden of Eden (Genesis 3:1–6) and when he attempted to mislead Jesus after his fast in the wilderness (Matthew 4:1–11). Even today, Satan masquerades as an "angel of light" (2 Corinthians 11:14). He is referred to as "the father of lies" with no truth in him (John 8:44 NIV). We are advised to "be sober, be vigilant; because your adversary the devil walks about like a roaring lion, seeking whom he may devour" (1 Peter 5:8).

By aligning ourselves with Christ, we can trust in God's greater power and resist Satan's attempts to undermine us (Luke 10:17–20; 1 John 4:4). Through submission to God, we are empowered to resist the devil, who will then flee (James 4:7). Satan will one day be defeated for good (Revelation 19:20; 20:7–10).

Demons, also referred to as evil spirits or unclean spirits, are also real. Demons are fallen angels, and the Bible acknowledges their existence (Revelation 12:3–4). They are sometimes associated with false gods (2 Chronicles 11:15; Deuteronomy 32:17).

Originally, demons were angels who were cast out of heaven after aligning with the devil rather than God. This event is depicted in Revelation 12:9: "The great dragon was cast out, that serpent of old, called the Devil and Satan, who deceives the whole world; he was cast to the earth, and his angels were cast out with him."

As followers of Satan, demons share his deceptive nature. Demons retain the power they had as angels, though it appears that God has placed some limitations on them (2 Thessalonians 2:6–7). Their influence is primarily spiritual, but they can sometimes influence or enter our physical world.

For instance, in Mark 5, Jesus encountered a man possessed by demons whose mental state led to severe physical and psychological turmoil. The man, who could not be restrained even with chains, displayed extraordinary strength likely granted by demons. Upon Jesus' intervention, the man's condition was transformed, and he was found "sitting there, dressed and in his right mind" (v. 15 NIV). While demons can affect physical conditions, not all physical issues are necessarily caused by demonic influence (Matthew 10:1; Luke 8:2).

Satan and demons are real, according to the Bible. We need to be aware of them, but we do not need to fear them when we have the Spirit of God at work in our lives.

91. CAN A CHRISTIAN BE POSSESSED BY A DEMON OR EVIL SPIRIT?

The Bible reveals several accounts when people were influenced or possessed by demons, but what about believers? Can a Christian ever be demon-possessed?

Christians can experience demonic oppression but not demon possession. There is a big difference. An evil spirit can still influence Christians to do wrong but cannot control a person in whom God's Spirit dwells.

The New Testament does not describe any instances of demons being cast out of believers; instead, Christians are instructed to resist the devil, which pertains to battling demonic influence rather than possession (Ephesians 6:10–18; James 4:7; 1 Peter 5:8–9).

For believers, possession is not possible because they are indwelt by the Holy Spirit (Romans 8:9–11; 1 Corinthians 3:16). The Holy Spirit, residing within believers, would not coexist with an evil spirit. It is inconsistent with the nature of God, who has redeemed believers with his own blood (1 Peter 1:18–19) and made them new creations in Christ (2 Corinthians 5:17; Ephesians 5:7–9).

While Christians are engaged in spiritual warfare against darkness, this darkness is not within them. First John 4:4 reassures us: "You are of God, little children, and have overcome them, because He who is in you is greater than he who is in the world." The Holy Spirit is described as "in us" whereas Satan and his demons are "in the world." Since believers have overcome the world, which is influenced by demons, these spirits cannot indwell them or control them.

Personal experiences and perceptions should not override the clear teachings of Scripture (2 Timothy 3:16–17; 2 Peter 1:19). It is possible for someone who appears to be a believer to not be genuinely saved (Matthew 7:21–23), but it is not biblically possible for a true Christian to be possessed by a demon.

Sometimes people use the example of the disciple Judas as evidence that a Christian can be possessed by a demon. The Bible says that "Satan entered Judas" (Luke 22:3). However, Jesus also predicted that Judas would betray him and said that Judas did not truly believe: "'But there are some of you who do not believe.' For Jesus knew from the beginning who they were who did not believe, and who would betray Him" (John 6:64).

If a Christian shows signs of what seems like demon possession, it is more likely that they are either not genuinely saved or are instead experiencing severe oppression. Sometimes, people also blame physical or mental health issues on demon possession. While some examples may involve both demonic possession and physical or mental health concerns, we believe that care must be taken to address physical and mental health issues separately. Physical and mental concerns are part of our fallen, imperfect world, and we must not automatically or uncritically blame them on demons.

Believers cannot be demon-possessed, though we still face spiritual warfare. We are to fight against spiritual forces of evil, knowing that we can defeat temptation by the power of the Spirit of God within us.

92. WHAT DOES THE BIBLE TEACH ABOUT ANGELS?

The Bible often speaks about angels, but what can we know about these spiritual beings?

Angels are distinct, created beings, fundamentally different from humans. People do not become angels after death, nor do angels ever become human. The difference between humans and angels is as significant as the difference between humans and animals. Angels are intelligent (Matthew 8:29), emotional (Luke 2:13), and possess individual personalities (Luke 8:28–31). They are spiritual entities (Hebrews 1:14) without physical bodies.

Angels are powerful but are created by God and must submit to him. Both benevolent and malevolent angels are created beings with limited knowledge (Matthew 24:36). Satan (formerly Lucifer) is a powerful angel, but he is not nearly as powerful as God.

Angels, however, are more powerful than humans and have a greater understanding of divine matters. They comprehend Scripture and believe in God's prophecies (James 2:19; Revelation 12:12). Even fallen angels acknowledge God's existence and are not atheistic (James 2:19; cf. Matthew 8:28–29). The number of angels is finite, and they do not reproduce. The number of angels created at the beginning remains as they were, and the fallen angels continue in their rebellion.

Given their enduring existence, angels likely possess more extensive knowledge of God and humanity than we do. When discussing fallen angels or demons, human accounts should not be the complete basis for our decisions. Instead, Scripture should be used to counter any deceptions. Accounts of human experiences can potentially be instructive, but Scripture should be the ultimate arbiter by which we measure the validity of all conclusions about spiritual matters.

Angels, like all created beings, are under God's authority. God dispatches holy angels to assist believers: "Are they not all ministering spirits sent forth to minister for those who will inherit salvation?" (Hebrews 1:14). They also engage in praising God (Psalm 148:1–2; Revelation 5:8–13) and serving him (Psalm 103:20). They are present before God (Job 1:6; 2:1), announce his judgments (Revelation 7:1; 8:2), minister to humans, and sometimes deliver answers to prayers. For example, in Acts 12, an angel rescued Peter from jail in response to the prayers of the apostle and other believers.

Angels also offer encouragement. During a storm, Paul told those on a ship with him, "There stood by me this night an angel of the God to whom I belong and whom I serve, saying, 'Do not be afraid, Paul; you must be brought before Caesar; and indeed God has granted you all those who sail with you'" (Acts 27:23–24).

The angels, at least sometimes, also care for believers at death. In Luke 16:22, Jesus said, "So it was that the beggar died, and was carried by the angels to Abraham's bosom."

Angels are unique from humans in many ways but share some traits. Angels and humans are both created by God, are designed to serve him, and are made to worship him.

SECTION 10

TECHNOLOGY AND THE END TIMES

93. WHAT DOES THE BIBLE SAY ABOUT AI (ARTIFICIAL INTELLIGENCE)?

In recent years, the rise in AI (artificial intelligence) has led to growing concerns for Christians. Does the Bible say anything about AI? What concerns should we have about its use in our society?

AI is the use of technology to automatically generate information or perform electronic tasks. For example, AI can be used to create images based on keywords or create written content based on parameters a user provides. AI can be used for good things, such as speeding up repetitive tasks or generating creative ideas. Others fear it could serve as part of an end-times deception or even a new world order.

Daniel 12:4 predicts, "You, Daniel, shut up the words, and seal the book until the time of the end; many shall run to and fro, and knowledge shall increase." These words clearly indicate an increase in information in the last days, though the details are not specified regarding AI.

Some areas of concern for today's Christians should include ethics. The use of AI in creating pornography or helping students cheat on tests or homework crosses lines regarding other biblical teachings. In addition, the controls involved in AI may pose concerns related to religious liberty and censorship. The media has already reported several examples of limited or inaccurate responses AI gives to ethical questions. These are due to the input humans give to the platform, input which may be biased toward a particular worldview or is simply not advanced enough to answer a particular request.

Others suggest that these AI tools will be used by the Antichrist in the tribulation to control society and individuals through deceptive practices. This will likely be true, as prophets predict the Antichrist will use his influence in many ways to deceive the world. The specifics are unknown, but we can expect his agenda will include the practice of using any available tools.

For right now, we need not fear AI but should have a healthy skepticism of its abilities, limitations, and even inaccuracies. Just as information on the internet or media can carry messages contrary to our biblical beliefs, AI has the potential to distort the truth either intentionally or unintentionally through controls its developers have put into place.

Our standard of truth must remain God's Word rather than any other source of information. We must use Scripture as our basis to evaluate other messages like those found through AI, using discernment to deal with the latest technologies that permeate our culture.

94. Is the Technology for Global Surveillance Now in Place?

One prediction about the future Antichrist is that he will have total control of world government. This has led to many questions about today's global surveillance and what technologies are currently in place.

Today's spy movies feature drones and other electronic tools that make it look like the government can find out everything about us at any moment. While films and novels take liberties and exaggerate for effect, there is a level of truth about the electronic controls in our world.

Most financial transactions are now digital. Without a digital transaction, it is almost impossible in Western nations to buy a car, purchase a home, receive an education, get a job, or receive many types of health care. Nearly every area of our lives is under the influence of electronic tools, which evil people could easily use in wrongful ways. One hack, publicized in the news in 2024, claimed that the social security numbers of every American had been shared on the dark web. If true, the exploit reveals that our lives are increasingly digital and can be misused by others in significant ways.

In Revelation 11, two witnesses who faithfully proclaimed God's message were put to death in Jerusalem at the midpoint of the tribulation. Verse 9 says, "Those from the peoples, tribes, tongues, and nations will see their dead bodies three-and-a-half days, and not allow their dead bodies to be put into graves." Many have taught that everyone in the world will have access to see this event. We once disagreed with this view, wondering how everyone could watch the same news at once. But today everyone with internet access can watch livestream views of cameras in Jerusalem. This is in addition to live news that provides 24/7 coverage of activities worldwide.

Because of the invasive nature of technology and global surveillance, a movement toward "off-grid" living has boomed in recent years. While there is certainly an appeal to get away from it all, God had called us to use our lives to impact others with the gospel.

Global surveillance has grown to concerning new levels; that is clear. We will always face the challenges of invasive technology in our lives but need not fear it. Our Lord is greater than anything we face. Peter gives the correct perspective: "Who is he who will harm you if you become followers of what is good? But even if you should suffer for righteousness' sake, you are blessed. 'And do not be afraid of their threats, nor be troubled'" (1 Peter 3:13–14).

95. Are RFID Technology or Similar Tracking Tools a Mark of the Beast?

The Bible predicts that during the tribulation, every person must take a mark on their right hand or forehead to buy or sell. Is RFID technology (radio frequency identification) for global surveillance in place today?

Revelation 13:16–17 mentions the mark of the beast that will be put into place during this future period: "He causes all, both small and great, rich and poor, free and slave, to receive a mark on their right hand or on their foreheads, and that no one may buy or sell except one who has the mark or the name of the beast, or the number of his name."

In one sense, a simple mark or tattoo could fulfill the biblical prediction, but today's technology makes this prediction even more frightening. For example, satellites such as Elon Musk's Starlink are making online connections available anywhere on the planet. While satellite phones already offer this technology, we are nearing the time when every person on the planet with a device could be connected.

Devices are also becoming more prevalent. Consider that the first iPhone was released in 2007. Today, you can buy a smartwatch or even smart glasses, and you can buy and sell with mobile apps at many locations without cash, debit card, or other form of physical payment. Some technologies are already experimenting with an RFID chip injected under their skin. On a less intrusive level, you can pay for your food at some stores by scanning your palm on a screen.

Over the past several decades, some people were concerned that the use of barcode scanners, credit cards, or the internet was some form of the mark of the beast. While this is not accurate, technology has continued to develop to the point that a small piece of technology can now be distributed to anyone on the planet and it can be connected to an online account that is centrally controlled and monitored. These tools will come under the control of the Antichrist during the tribulation period that follows the rapture, allowing worldwide control of the marketplace.

While Christians today do not need to be scared of accidentally taking the mark of the beast through some form of technology, we should be concerned about our personal safety, security, and religious freedoms in the ongoing infiltration of technology in our lives. Some of these tools can be helpful to our daily lives, we should closely evaluate others, and when necessary, we should reject any that impose unwanted surveillance.

96. What does the Bible teach about a global currency? Does this involve cryptocurrency?

Many prophecy teachers speak about a future global government with a single currency. What does the Bible teach about finances in the future, and does this involve the growth of cryptocurrency?

The Bible does not explicitly mention a one-world currency, but it does present concepts that align with these ideas. For instance, the future Antichrist will wield significant global influence. Revelation 13:3–4 describes this figure: "I saw one of his heads as if it had been mortally wounded, and his deadly wound was healed. And all the world marveled and followed the beast. So they worshiped the dragon who gave authority to the beast; and they worshiped the beast, saying, 'Who is like the beast? Who is able to make war with him?'"

The Antichrist will possess considerable power and control on a global scale. Revelation 13:7–8 states, "It was granted to him to make war with the saints and to overcome them. And authority was given him over every tribe, tongue, and nation. All who dwell on the earth will worship him, whose names have not been written in the Book of Life of the Lamb slain from the foundation of the world." This passage suggests widespread allegiance to the Antichrist, though it does not specifically confirm the existence of a one-world currency.

During the tribulation, allegiance to the Antichrist will be compulsory for all people to buy or sell: "No one may buy or sell except one who has the mark or the name of the beast, or the number of his name" (v. 17). This future time during the tribulation indicates that a mark for conducting business will be required.

Today, transactions can occur across various currencies using credit cards and online platforms. A single currency is not essential for fulfilling the prophecy about the mark of the beast, though it remains a possibility.

Some have suggested that our growing cashless society or even cryptocurrency is part of this trend moving toward a global currency under the control of a single leader. For those unfamiliar with it, cryptocurrency is a digital form of payment that uses cryptography (encryption) to secure transactions.

Cryptocurrency was originally used to help users make anonymous payments. Now, various cryptocurrencies are also used as an alternative to government-backed funds like the US dollar or the Euro, allowing users to make exchanges without depending on a federal government.

The use of cryptocurrency is not associated with the mark of the beast. However, during the future tribulation, a single ruler will require all people to take a mark to buy or sell. Today's financial tools and technologies show that such a system could be put into place, adding a sense of urgency regarding the rapture that will occur at any moment before these events during the tribulation.

97. How Should Christians (Especially Parents) View the Internet and Social Media?

Many parents have asked us for advice on how to handle the use of the internet and social media for their children. The Bible was written long before these technologies but does address important principles concerning their use and the responsibility of parents to protect their children.

The most important principle is to model what you want to see in your children. For example, if, as a parent, you spend all of your waking hours looking at a screen, you should not be surprised to see your children copy your behavior. How much technology you consume, which forms you embrace, and the ways in which you use it impacts your kids more than anything else.

Second, you are responsible for protecting your child from online harm. This includes setting up blocks against pornography and violent content, blocking inappropriate movies on streaming services, and monitoring their usage. As a parent, you should be able to check the browsing history of your child to make sure there is some accountability both for what they watch and for how long they are consuming content.

Third, guard key times of temptation. For example, keeping devices out of your child's bedroom after a certain time of night is an appropriate and easy way to stop late-night viewing of harmful content. Some parents also shut down their Wi-Fi after a certain time to stop late-night usage by children.

Fourth, regularly talk with your children about what they are watching online, including having biblical discussions about life. Deuteronomy 6:6–9 teaches, "These words which

I command you today shall be in your heart. You shall teach them diligently to your children, and shall talk of them when you sit in your house, when you walk by the way, when you lie down, and when you rise up. You shall bind them as a sign on your hand, and they shall be as frontlets between your eyes. You shall write them on the doorposts of your house and on your gates."

A close look at these ideas from Deuteronomy helps us still today. For example, we are called to teach God's words to our children throughout the day. This includes when we sit in the house, such as during meals.

We can talk when we travel, whether on foot, in a vehicle, or even on an airplane. We can also talk together about spiritual things before bedtime and pray together to help build positive, godly input into the lives of our children. Scripture also encourages us to begin our day focused on God, whether in prayer, devotions, or both (Psalm 1:2; 5:3; 90:14; 143:8; Mark 1:35).

We can also apply other aspects of this passage. For example, the idea of writing out Bible verses and displaying them in prominent places (such as on a poster on their bedroom wall or even on the background of a phone, tablet, or computer screen) can help our kids. Clothing and accessories, such as Christian T-shirts, jewelry, hats, and similar items can encourage us and remind our children of God's ways.

Today's technologies can be challenging, but this does not allow us to give up our roles as parents who protect, guide, encourage, instruct, and, in some cases, correct when it comes to the use of the internet and social media.

98. Will the Beast of Revelation Be a Computer-Generated Entity?

Today's rise of artificial intelligence and computer-generated images has led to many questions about its misuse during the end times. Some have asked whether the beast of Revelation will be a computer-generated entity.

During the tribulation, one of the functions of the second beast, known as the false prophet, will be to mislead people into creating an image of the first beast. Revelation 13:14–15 says:

> He deceives those who dwell on the earth by those signs which he was granted to do in the sight of the beast, telling those who dwell on the earth to make an image to the beast who was wounded by the sword and lived. He was granted power to give breath to the image of the beast, that the image of the beast should both speak and cause as many as would not worship the image of the beast to be killed.

The false prophet will animate the image of the first beast, making it capable of demanding worship. People will be required to worship this image and receive the beast's mark on their foreheads or hands to engage in commerce. Those who refuse will face execution.

Historically, scholars envisioned this image as a statue with a lifelike appearance. However, with advancements in technology, some now speculate that it could be some form of technology. For example, artificial intelligence can copy a person's voice, mimic a person's video image, and say whatever a person programs the image to say.

Various holograms and avatars have also become popular. In Japan, Vocaloids have become part of the culture. Vocaloids are voice synthesizers that are matched with an animated character. Such animations are now common in games, cartoons, music videos, and other media. With today's video projection systems and even hologram systems, which make the images of people from the past appear very lifelike, it would not be surprising to find that the future image of the beast will include some sort of computer-generated image.

However, this is a development that will occur during the tribulation, which we understand will follow the rapture of believers that will take place at any moment (1 Corinthians 15:51–58; 1 Thessalonians 4:13–18). The timing of the image of the beast means that today's believers do not need to worry about accidentally worshiping the image of the beast or taking the mark of the beast. Instead, we can view developments in technology as a warning of how soon God's prophecies could unfold. Our application must be to share Christ with others and to be prepared through a daily commitment to the Lord.

Despite not knowing its exact form, the image of the beast in the future will be central to the worship of the Antichrist. We are called to worship the Lord and to have no other gods before us, both now and in the future.

99. Do Modern Alien or UFO Sightings Have Anything to Do with the End Times?

After the rapture, a seven-year period of tribulation will occur. This raises questions about how those left on earth will be deceived into rejecting Jesus despite the dramatic event of many people disappearing. One theory is that an alien deception will explain this phenomenon. Is this possible?

Matthew 24:24 indicates that a significant deception will occur that will lead many to reject Jesus despite the rapture. The Bible, however, does not specify the nature of this deception. With the perpetual popularity of aliens and UFOs in our culture, it is plausible that some might attribute the disappearance of individuals to alien activity.

Theories involving aliens have been around for a long time. It's reasonable to assume that some explanations for the rapture could involve aliens. Much of this deception will likely be orchestrated by Satan and the Antichrist, as Paul describes in 2 Thessalonians 2:9–12:

> The coming of the lawless one is according to the working of Satan, with all power, signs, and lying wonders, and with all unrighteous deception among those who perish, because they did not receive the love of the truth, that they might be saved. And for this reason God will send them strong delusion, that they should believe the lie, that they all may be condemned who did not believe the truth but had pleasure in unrighteousness.

It's also conceivable that demons might impersonate extraterrestrial beings to spread deceit, an idea some associate with Genesis 6:4.

Although the exact nature of this deception is uncertain, Christians should be aware of the possibility. Even within churches, discussions about aliens are not uncommon, often in a humorous or speculative context. The widespread acceptance of the idea of alien life could influence future explanations for the rapture.

For instance, some might view the rapture as an alien abduction, a concept that has been proposed by various individuals over the years. For example, the Marvel Avengers films include a disappearance called the Snap or the Blip, which made half of all humanity disappear. In addition, secular scientists have increasingly promoted ideas like the multiverse or extraterrestrial origins of life. As such theories gain traction, they could influence the future world's interpretation of events like the rapture.

While this is speculative, it highlights the possibility that alien deception could be one of the proposed explanations for the rapture. What remains most important for us is our present faith in Jesus Christ for salvation and sharing this message with others.

100. Is There Really a "Deep State," and Could It Have Prophetic Implications?

The idea of a deep state is the view that influential members of government or society control the nation or world. Does our nation's growing concern about a deep state have prophetic connections?

In one sense, it clearly does. The Bible predicts a future global leader called the Antichrist who will lead much of the world, its commerce, government, and religion. Those who oppose him will face persecution and death. The rise of a more controlling federal government, whether in the US or in other nations, points to this future time when globalism will be in full force. Those who do not comply will face serious consequences.

Thankfully, the Antichrist will arise during the tribulation, a time that follows the rapture of believers. Those who know the Lord will be with him and escape this future time of control. However, those who remain will face difficult times, both due to government control and natural disasters.

In another sense, American Christians also realize the importance of limited government and its relationship to our freedom of religion. When there are fewer government regulations, individual believers and churches enjoy more freedom to worship God and serve others. When the government adds more restrictions, this freedom becomes more limited, leading to the potential persecution of unliked religious groups.

The founding fathers of America and early pioneers often moved to this nation to escape religious persecution in other nations. Our country's freedoms sought to provide protections for citizens to worship God freely, a privilege many take for granted today.

A look back at the context of the New Testament is also helpful. The apostles and early believers lived under the control of the Roman Empire. They did not enjoy the religious liberty that Americans do today but instead faced times of intense persecution. Despite being persecuted, the church grew and flourished.

Their example is insightful for our times. If we face more problems from federal and global regulations, we are called to continue to live for Christ and know that our faith can continue to thrive despite persecution. We do not desire a loss of our religious liberties but recognize that God works despite any limitations we face.

In Acts 4:19–20, Peter and John were commanded to stop teaching about Jesus. They responded, "Whether it is right in the sight of God to listen to you more than to God, you judge. For we cannot but speak the things which we have seen and heard." The prophet Daniel also faced death for refusing to stop offering his prayers to the Lord. He was saved from the den of lions (Daniel 6). His three friends Shadrach, Meshach, and Abednego refused to bow down to other gods, and the Lord saved them from a fiery furnace (Daniel 3).

The Lord calls us to faithfulness despite the context of the government or world around us. When we remain faithful, we can rejoice in suffering: "When you do good and suffer, if you take it patiently, this is commendable before God. For to this you were called, because Christ also suffered for us, leaving us an example, that you should follow His steps" (1 Peter 2:20–21).

THE ULTIMATE QUESTION

People everywhere invest their lives in the search for meaning, purpose, and fulfillment. But people need something more than money, fame, luxurious houses, good looks, nice cars, or a lucrative stock portfolio. There is nothing necessarily wrong with these things, but they cannot provide peace to the soul or forgiveness of one's sin.

I once read that the highest rates of suicide and divorce occur among the most affluent classes of society. On the West Coast, psychologists and counselors have isolated a new affliction and have given it a name: "Sudden Acquired Wealth Syndrome." People are achieving every benchmark that our society says should make them happy, but they are finding that it is possible to be materially rich yet spiritually bankrupt. Many people have a schedule that is full but a heart that is empty.

Several years ago, our nine-member ministry team crossed America on a fifty-states-in-fifty-days trip. During this journey across America, I preached in every service we attended, and I personally talked with thousands of people. We had the privilege of hosting sixty-four worship services throughout the entire United States. Our outreach team met many people who came to us with probing questions and genuine concern about spiritual issues. People today truly are looking for meaningful answers, craving hope in a dangerous world.

Present realities, such as worldwide terrorist attacks, global economic uncertainty, political instability, and natural disasters like Hurricane Katrina and COVID-19 have only intensified this search.

Immediately after the terrorist attacks of 9/11, I (Alex) went to New York City to help with a prayer center that the Billy Graham ministry and Samaritan's Purse had set up. Just like on my fifty-state tour, I was talking daily to hundreds of people from every background imaginable. They may have expressed themselves in different ways, but they all had the same basic question: *Who is God, and how may I come to know him?*

Where one stands with God is the most vital of all issues, but the good news is that you may settle this today! You may have wondered, *How does a person become a Christian? How can I be certain that my sin is forgiven? How may I experience consistent spiritual growth?* Let's consider these things together.

God's Word Explains the Message of Salvation

Jesus said in John 3:3, "No one can see the kingdom of God unless they are born again" (NIV). Salvation is the issue: The most important question you will ever ask yourself is this: *Do I know for certain that I have eternal life and that I will go to heaven when I die?*

If you stood before God right now and he asked, "Why should I let you into my heaven?", what would you say?

The Bible describes our condition: "All have sinned and fall short of the glory of God" (Romans 3:23 NIV). Just as a job pays a wage at the end of the week, our sins will yield a result at the end of a lifetime: "The wages of sin is death [the Bible describes this as separation from God, the punishment of hell], but the gift of God is eternal life in Christ Jesus our Lord" (6:23 NIV).

God shows his love for you personally by his provision for your need: "God demonstrates his own love for us in this: While we were still sinners, Christ died for us" (Romans 5:8 NIV).

Salvation requires repentance, which means a "turning." Jesus said, "Unless you repent, you too will all perish" (Luke 13:3

NIV). The New Testament emphasizes the necessity of repentance "so that your sins may be wiped out" (Acts 3:19 NIV).

Every one of us has sinned, and the Bible says that our sins must be dealt with. We have a twofold sin problem. We are sinners by birth, and we are sinners by choice. Somebody once said to Dr. Vance Havner, "This thing about man's sin nature, I find that hard to swallow." The great evangelist responded, "You don't have to swallow it—you're born with it; it's already in you."[9]

The world classifies sin, viewing some things as worse than others. But the Bible teaches that all sin is an offense against God, and even one sin is serious enough to keep someone out of heaven. You may not have robbed a bank (or maybe you have). God doesn't grade on a curve; humanity is a tainted race, and sin is the problem.

Oftentimes in life, we know what is right, but we do what is wrong. You may have even looked back at yourself and wondered, *What was I thinking? Why did I do that? How could I have said that?* Jesus said that man needs to repent and make a change. Repentance means turning from your sins and to Christ. By faith, trust who Jesus is (God's Son and mankind's Savior) and what Jesus did (died in your place and rose from the dead).

We receive God's forgiveness by faith. We are to confess our faith before others, not be ashamed to let the world know that we believe in Jesus: "If you declare with your mouth, 'Jesus is Lord,' and believe in your heart that God raised him from the dead, you will be saved. For it is with your heart that you believe and are justified, and it is with your mouth that you profess your faith and are saved" (Romans 10:9–10 NIV).

---

9 Southern Baptist Evangelists, "God Loves You!," accessed March 25, 2021, https://www.sbcevangelist.org.

What is faith? Faith is trust. It is simple, honest, child-like trust. God says that you have a sin problem but that he loves you and will forgive you. God says that through Jesus Christ, he has made a way for anyone to be saved who will come to him. Do you trust what God has said and what God has done? If you come to Christ in belief and faith, God promises to save you: "Everyone who calls on the name of the Lord will be saved" (v. 13 NIV). Jesus promises: "Whoever comes to me I will never drive away" (John 6:37 NIV).

During the fifty-state evangelistic tour, we gave away thousands of yellow stickers that said, "Jesus Saves, Pray Today!" That is not a trite saying or marketing cliché. It is a deep biblical truth, and if you desire to have a relationship with the Lord, you can enter Christ's salvation through faith right where you are now. Make your journey to the cross today through this basic prayer of commitment:

Dear Lord Jesus, I know that I have sinned, and I cannot save myself. I believe that you are the Son of God and that you died and rose again for me in order to forgive my sins and to be my Savior. I turn from my sins, and I ask you to forgive me. I receive you into my heart as my Lord and Savior. Jesus, thank you for saving me now. Help me to live the rest of my life for you. Amen.

GOD'S WORD GIVES YOU ASSURANCE OF SALVATION

You can overcome doubts about where you stand with God. Based on what God's Word says (not what you feel or assume), you can know that you have eternal life: "Whoever has the Son has life; whoever does not have the Son of God does not have life. I write these things to you who believe in the name of the Son of God so that you may know that you have eternal life" (1 John 5:12–13 NIV).

Jesus said, "Whoever hears my word and believes him who sent me has eternal life and will not be judged but has crossed over from death to life" (John 5:24 NIV). Remember: you are not saved by good works, and you are not "kept saved" by good works. Your merit before God is totally based on Jesus; God credits Christ's perfection, holiness, and righteousness to each one who believes by faith.

WHAT DOES THE TERM "REDEDICATION" MEAN?

While speaking at churches and Christian events around the nation, we encourage people to give their lives fully to Christ. Often in calling people to a Christian commitment, we ask if anyone in the audience needs to *rededicate* their life to God.

A man recently asked what this term *rededication* meant. "Rededication" is for a believer who desires to renew and deepen their walk with Christ. A Christian can wander from God in sin or simply lose their closeness to the Lord through the busyness of life.

If you are a born-again Christian, you are forever God's child. Your salvation is a matter of adoption, sometimes referred to as sonship. Your daily Christian growth is a matter of fellowship. Your spiritual birth into God's family is, in some ways, similar to your physical birth into the human family. For instance, as a young child, you may have disobeyed and disappointed your parents. Something you did may have grieved your parents, but you were still their child because you had been born into that family.

In the same way, the Christian's relationship to the Lord is still intact even though a sin we commit may hinder our daily fellowship with God. Salvation is a one-time, instantaneous event; Christian growth and personal fellowship with God is an everyday, lifelong process. Consistent daily prayer, Bible study, obedience to the Holy Spirit, and nurturing in a local church fellowship are all keys to growth and Christian maturity.

While your "sonship" may be intact, your daily "fellowship" may be lacking. Christ, not self, must be on the throne of your heart and life. Sin hinders our fellowship with God. "Your iniquities have separated you from your God; your sins have hidden his face from you, so that he will not hear" (Isaiah 59:2 NIV). Perhaps your desire is like that of David after he had wandered from God: "Create in me a pure heart, O God, and renew a steadfast spirit within me" (Psalm 51:10 NIV).

God lovingly receives all who turn to him and all who return to him. He cleanses us from sin and restores us to fellowship with him. King David had been "a man after [God's] own heart" (1 Samuel 13:14 NIV), but his sinful deeds required that he humbly re-commit himself to the Lord: "Do not cast me from your presence...Restore to me the joy of your salvation" (Psalm 51:11–12 NIV).

Christian publications often use the following verse in the context of evangelism, and that is okay, but 1 John 1:9 is really a promise to the Christian who needs to make things right with the Lord: "If we confess our sins, he is faithful and just and will forgive us our sins and purify us from all unrighteousness" (NIV). From the same chapter is another great truth that gives us precious, sweet assurance: "If we walk in the light, as he is in the light, we have fellowship with one another, and the blood of Jesus, his Son, purifies us from all sin" (v. 7 NIV).

You may already know the Lord but wish to pray these basic words of rededication and commitment:

Lord Jesus, I acknowledge that I have sinned and wandered from you. I confess my sin and turn from it. I recommit myself to you as Lord. Thank you for forgiving me. I trust you to give me the strength to live for you each day of my life. Thank you for being my Savior, my Lord, and my friend. Amen.

May God bless you as you journey on with him. If you have made a decision for Christ just now, it would be my honor to hear from you. If you do not have a Bible and would like to request one or if you have other questions or spiritual needs, write to:

Dr. Alex McFarland
c/o Alex McFarland Evangelistic Ministries
P.O. Box 10231
Greensboro, NC 27404
Or email us through the website at alexmcfarland.com.

ABOUT THE AUTHORS

ALEX MCFARLAND is an evangelist, author, and advocate for Christian apologetics. Cohost of *Exploring the Word* with Bert Harper (heard nationally on the American Family Radio Network), Alex is the founder and president of the national apologetic conference Truth for a New Generation. He has served as president of Southern Evangelical Seminary and Director of Teen Apologetics for *Focus on the Family* under James Dobson. He has served as adjunct professor at several Christian universities, assisting with the creation of programs and departments dedicated to apologetics and the defense of the Christian worldview. Alex is the author of many books, including the best-selling *10 Most Common Objections to Christianity*. He is a graduate of Liberty University. Alex and his wife Angela live in North Carolina.

BERT HARPER is the director of Marriage, Family, and Pastoral Ministries at the American Family Association. He has served as cohost of *Exploring the Word* with Alex McFarland for more than a decade and is heard on an average of two hundred stations nationwide each weekday. As a pastor of local churches, Bert has nearly four decades of experience counseling couples. He has faithfully served on the board of the American Family Association and Blue Mountain College, and he has fulfilled many other leadership roles on behalf of churches and Christian organizations. Together, he and his wife Jan lead marriage conferences and retreats for ministers and their wives. The Harpers have three grown sons and are the proud grandparents of a growing family.

PRAISE FOR *EXPLORING THE WORD*

I love listening to *Exploring the Word* on my way home from work, and it's a literal blessing to have this book from Pastor Bert and Dr. Alex. I say that because a blessing is something that comes to you, fills your cup, and then overflows to others. Being able to read and study these Scripture-based answers fills me up and then helps me spread the knowledge of God and his Word to the people I interact with daily.

—Tyler S., Columbus, OH

Bert and Alex, I have listened to your shows for years and have gained so much practical wisdom. Your insights on Scripture deeply touch my life.

—Charles C., Richmond, VA

Exploring the Word has been a part of our daily afternoon drive for many years. Our kids have grown up listening to Alex McFarland and Bert Harper, and our whole family has a knowledge of the Bible thanks to your show.

—Erin S., MS

Thank you for your practical wisdom and kindness shown to all callers. You both treat the listeners respectfully—no matter the question—and that really says a lot.

—Linda L., Seattle, WA

I don't consider myself a religious person—in fact, I'm a bit of a skeptic regarding religion. But I tend to trust what Alex and Bert present on *Exploring the Word*. Not only do they back up their answers with facts, but they also speak with such conviction that it is hard not to trust what they say.

—Tom B., Chicago, IL